"*THE WAY OF A PILGRIM is unique among devotional books. It has a special purity and simplicity of spirit.* Parts of John Woolman's *Journal,* and the writings of Brother Lawrence, are the closest analogies to the chronicle of the wanderings and spiritual adventures of this unknown 19th-century Russian pilgrim. His spontaneous ministry of love to his fellow men, his earnest wrestlings with the problem of how to pray continually, his humble receptiveness to the promptings of God become a shared religious experience with the reader. It is wholly accessible to persons unschooled in formal theology or complex mystical devotions."

—EDMUND FULLER

THE WAY
OF A PILGRIM

and

The Pilgrim Continues
His Way

Translated from the Russian by

R. M. FRENCH

BALLANTINE BOOKS • NEW YORK

SBN 345-24254-8-150

This edition published by arrangement with
The Seabury Press.

First Printing: November, 1974

Printed in the United States of America

BALLANTINE BOOKS
A Division of Random House, Inc.
201 East 50th Street, New York, N.Y. 10022

To the Reader

TRY a little journey with this Pilgrim; for you will find him very good company. You probably will not always agree with his naïve talk; but your differences from his outlook will afford much fruit for reflection in the silences which he so greatly values: and in any case you will appreciate his entire simplicity and sincerity.

He harps very much on one string, no doubt; but what a string it is!—a deep bourbon-sound, which runs on, underneath the harmonies and discords of daily life, till it has brought them into unison with God.

If that ever seems monotonous, at any rate there is variety and charm in the vivid pictures of Russian life which illustrate his theme. They suggest a comparison with the matchless folk tales of Leo Tolstoi; and they do not suffer by such a comparison.

For the religion is sounder. Tolstoi wrote as the artist, who, in spite of his own morbid and restless mind, could depict what he saw and heard, but did not really *know*. Our pilgrim *knows* every bit of what he says: and you will listen, even to the strangest things that he says, with the respect which is due to real, vital knowledge.

I think you will be sorry when, at the end, he suddenly disappears into the obscurity from which he emerged when you first came across him.

WALTERUS TRURON.

Introduction

THE Russian title of this book may be literally translated "Candid Narratives of a Pilgrim to His Spiritual Father." The title chosen for the English version explains itself and is meant to cover the twofold interest of the book. It is the story of some of the Pilgrim's experiences as he made his *way* from place to place in Russia and Siberia. No one can miss the charm of these travel notes in the simple directness with which they are told and the clear-cut sketches of people which they contain.

It is also the story of the Pilgrim's learning and practising, and on occasion teaching to others, a *way* of praying. Upon this, the *hesychast* method of prayer, much might be said, and not everyone will be in sympathy with it. But everyone will appreciate the sincerity of his conviction and few probably will doubt the reality of his experience. Strongly contrasted as the method may be with an ordinary religious Englishman's habits of devotion, for another type of soul it may still be the expression of vivid realisation of the truth "for me to live is Christ."

Those who wish to read more of the *hesychast* method of prayer and its connection with the great Byzantine Mystic, St. Simeon the New Theologian, who lived from 949 to 1022, may be referred to *Orientalia Christiana,* Vol. IX, No. 36 (June and July, 1927).

The events described in the book appear to belong to a Russia prior to the Liberation of the Serfs, which took place in 1861. The reference to the Crimean War in the *Fourth Narrative* gives 1853 as the other limit of time. Between those two dates the Pilgrim arrived at Irkutsk, where he found a Spiritual Father. He tells the latter how he came to learn the Prayer of Jesus, partly from the oral teaching of his *starets,* and after the loss of his *starets,* from his own study of *The Philokalia.* This is the substance of the first two *Narratives,* which are divided by the death of the *starets.*

The *Third Narrative* is very short, and tells, in response to his Spiritual Father's enquiries, the Pilgrim's earlier personal history and what led him to become a Pilgrim at all.

It was his intention to go on from Irkutsk to Jerusalem, and indeed he had actually started. But a chance encounter led to a postponement of his departure for some days, and during that time he relates the further experiences of his pilgrim life which make up the *Fourth Narrative.*

Of the Pilgrim's identity nothing is known. In some way his manuscript, or a copy of it, came into the hands of a monk on Mount Athos, in whose possession it was found by the Abbot of St. Michael's Monastery at Kazan. The Abbot copied the manuscript, and from his copy the book was printed at Kazan in 1884.

In recent years copies of this (until April, 1930, the only) edition have become exceedingly difficult to get. There appear to be only three or four copies in existence outside Russia, and I am deeply indebted to friends in Denmark and Bulgaria for the loan of copies from which this translation was made. I am very grateful also to the Reverend N. Behr, Proto-priest of the Russian Church in London, for so kindly reading through the manuscript of my translation.

A very few notes have been added and placed at the end of the book. They are chiefly to explain one or two words which it seemed best not to attempt to turn into English.

R. M. F.

Note to Second Edition

"THE WAY of a Pilgrim" was first published in 1930. Its sequel, "The Pilgrim Continues his Way", came into my hands later and was published separately. The two are now issued as one continuous narrative.

I have added a few more short biographical notes on the Eastern Fathers who are mentioned in the text. All the biographical notes are now printed apart from the other notes and in alphabetical order.

Hampstead, 1952

R. M. F.

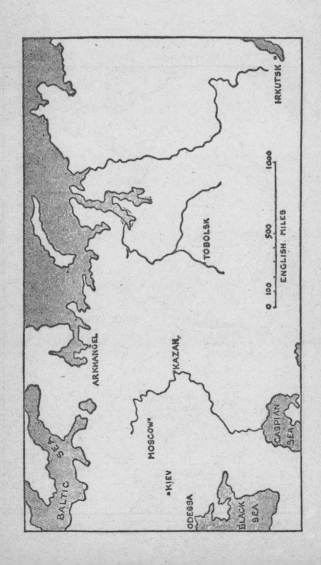

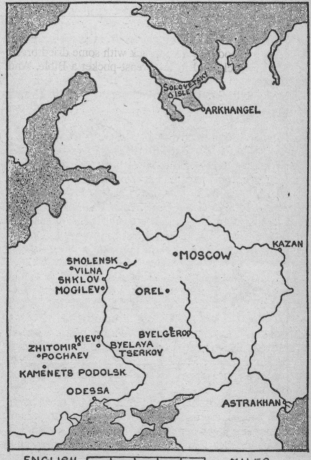

1

By the grace of God I am a Christian man, by my actions a great sinner, and by calling a homeless wanderer of the humblest birth who roams from place to place. My worldly goods are a knapsack with some dried bread in it on my back, and in my breast-pocket a Bible. And that is all.

On the 24th Sunday after Pentecost I went to church to say my prayers there during the Liturgy. The first Epistle of St. Paul to the Thessalonians was being read, and among other words I heard these—*"Pray without ceasing."* It was this text, more than any other, which forced itself upon my mind, and I began to think how it was possible to pray without ceasing, since a man has to concern himself with other things also in order to make a living. I looked at my Bible, and with my own eyes read the words which I had heard, *i.e.,* that we ought always, at all times and in all places, to pray with uplifted hands. I thought and thought, but knew not what to make of it. "What ought I to do?" I thought. "Where shall I find someone to explain it to me? I will go to the churches where famous preachers are to be heard; perhaps there I shall hear something which will throw light on it for me." I did so. I heard a number of very fine sermons on prayer; what prayer is, how much we need it, and what its fruits are; but no one said how one could succeed in prayer. I heard a sermon on spiritual prayer, and unceasing prayer, but how it was to be done was not pointed out.

Thus listening to sermons failed to give me what I wanted, and having had my fill of them without gaining understanding, I gave up going to hear public sermons. I settled on another plan—by God's help to look for some experienced and skilled person who would give me in conversation that teaching about unceasing prayer which drew me so urgently.

For a long time I wandered through many places. I read my Bible always, and everywhere I asked whether there was not in the neighbourhood a spiritual teacher, a devout and experienced guide, to be found. One day I was told that in a certain village a gentleman had long been living and seeking the salvation of his soul. He had a chapel in his house. He never left his estate, and he spent his time in prayer and reading devotional books. Hearing this, I ran rather than walked to the village named. I got there and found him.

"What do you want of me?" he asked.

"I have heard that you are a devout and clever person," said I. "In God's name please explain to me the meaning of the Apostle's words, '*Pray without ceasing.*' How is it possible to pray without ceasing? I want to know so much, but I cannot understand it at all."

He was silent for a while and looked at me closely. Then he said: "Ceaseless interior prayer is a continual yearning of the human spirit towards God. To succeed in this consoling exercise we must pray more often to God to teach us to pray without ceasing. Pray more, and pray more fervently. It is prayer itself which will reveal to you how it can be achieved unceasingly; but it will take some time."

So saying, he had food brought to me, gave me money for my journey, and let me go.

He did not explain the matter.

Again I set off. I thought and thought, I read and read, I dwelt over and over again upon what this man had said to me, but I could not get to the bottom of it. Yet so greatly did I wish to understand that I could not sleep at night.

I walked at least a hundred and twenty-five miles, and then I came to a large town, a provincial capital, where I saw a monastery. At the inn where I stopped I heard it said that the Abbot was a man of great kindness, devout and hospitable. I went to see him. He met me in a very friendly manner, asked me to sit down, and offered me refreshment.

"I do not need refreshment, holy Father," I said, "but I beg you to give me some spiritual teaching. How can I save my soul?"

"What? Save your soul? Well, live according to the commandments, say your prayers, and you will be saved."

"But I hear it said that we should pray without ceasing, and I don't know how to pray without ceasing. I cannot even understand what unceasing prayer means. I beg you, Father, explain this to me."

"I don't know how to explain further, dear brother. But, stop a moment, I have a little book, and it is explained there." And he handed me St. Dmitri's book on *The Spiritual Education of the Inner Man,* saying, "Look, read this page."

I began to read as follows: "The words of the Apostle *'Pray without ceasing'* should be understood as referring to the creative prayer of the understanding. The understanding can always be reaching out towards God, and pray to Him unceasingly."

"But," I asked, "what is the method by which the understanding can always be turned towards God, never be disturbed, and pray without ceasing?"

"It is very difficult, even for one to whom God Himself gives such a gift," replied the Abbot.

He did not give me the explanation.

I spent the night at his house, and in the morning, thanking him for his kindly hospitality, I went on my way; where to, I did not know myself. My failure to understand made me sad, and by way of comforting myself I read my Bible. In this way I followed the main road for five days.

At last towards evening I was overtaken by an old man who looked like a cleric of some sort. In answer to my question he told me that he was a monk belonging to a monastery some six miles off the main road. He asked me to go there with him. "We take in pilgrims," said he, "and give them rest and food with devout persons in the guest house." I did not feel like going. So in reply I said that my peace of mind in no way depended upon my finding a resting-place, but upon finding spiritual teaching. Neither was I running after food, for I had plenty of dried bread in my knapsack.

"What sort of spiritual teaching are you wanting to get?" he asked me. "What is it puzzling you? Come now! Do come to our house, dear brother. We have *startsi*[1]* of ripe experience well able to give guidance to your soul and to set it upon the true path, in the light of the word of God and the writings of the holy Fathers."

"Well, it's like this, Father", said I. "About a year ago, while I was at the Liturgy, I heard a passage from the Epistles which bade men pray without ceasing. Failing to understand, I began to read my Bible, and there also in many places I found the divine command that we ought to pray at all times, in all places; not only while about our business, not only while awake, but even during sleep, '*I sleep, but my heart waketh.*' This surprised me very much, and I was at a loss to understand how it could be carried out and in what way it was to be done. A burning desire and thirst for knowledge awoke in me. Day and night the matter was never out of my mind. So I began to go to churches and to listen to sermons. But however many I heard, from not one of them did I get any teaching about how to pray without ceasing. They always talked about getting ready for prayer, or about its fruits and the like, without teaching one *how* to pray without ceasing, or what such prayer means. I have often read the Bible and there made sure of what I have heard. But meanwhile I have not reached the understanding that I long for, and so to this hour I am still uneasy and in doubt."

Then the old man crossed himself and spoke. "Thank God, my dear brother, for having revealed to you this unappeasable desire for unceasing interior prayer. Recognise in it the call of God, and calm yourself. Rest assured that what has hitherto been accomplished in you is

* The number refers to the notes at the end of the book.
[1] *Starets,* pl. *startsi.* A monk distinguished by his great piety, long experience of the spiritual life, and gift for guiding other souls. Lay folk frequently resort to *startsi* for spiritual counsel; and in a monastery a new member of the community is attached to a *starets,* who trains and teaches him.

the testing of the harmony of your own will with the
voice of God. It has been granted to you to understand
that the heavenly light of unceasing interior prayer is attained neither by the wisdom of this world, nor by the
mere outward desire for knowledge, but that on the contrary it is found in poverty of spirit and in active experience in simplicity of heart. That is why it is not surprising that you have been unable to hear anything about
the essential work of prayer, and to acquire the knowledge by which ceaseless activity in it is attained. Doubt-
less a great deal has been preached about prayer, and
there is much about it in the teaching of various writers.
But since for the most part all their reasonings are based
upon speculation and the working of natural wisdom,
and not upon active experience, they sermonise about
the qualities of prayer, rather than about the nature of
the thing itself. One argues beautifully about the necessity of prayer, another about its power and the blessings
which attend it, a third again about the things which
lead to perfection in prayer, *i.e.*, about the absolute necessity of zeal, an attentive mind, warmth of heart, purity of thought, reconciliation with one's enemies, humility, contrition, and so on. But what is prayer? And how
does one learn to pray? Upon these questions, primary
and essential as they are, one very rarely gets any precise enlightenment from present-day preachers. For these
questions are more difficult to understand than all their
arguments that I have just spoken of, and require mystical knowledge, not simply the learning of the schools.
And the most deplorable thing of all is that the vain wisdom of the world compels them to apply the human
standard to the divine. Many people reason quite the
wrong way round about prayer, thinking that good actions and all sorts of preliminary measures render us capable of prayer. But quite the reverse is the case, it is
prayer which bears fruit in good works and all the virtues. Those who reason so, take, incorrectly, the fruits
and the results of prayer for the means of attaining it,
and this is to depreciate the power of prayer. And it is
quite contrary to Holy Scripture, for the Apostle Paul
says, '*I exhort therefore that first of all supplications be
made*' (1 Tim., ii, 1). The first thing laid down in the

Apostle's words about prayer is that the work of prayer comes before everything else: '*I exhort therefore that first of all . . .*' The Christian is bound to perform many good works, but before all else what he ought to do is to pray, for without prayer no other good work whatever can be accomplished. Without prayer he cannot find the way to the Lord, he cannot understand the truth, he cannot crucify the flesh with its passions and lusts, his heart cannot be enlightened with the light of Christ, he cannot be savingly united to God. None of those things can be effected unless they are preceded by constant prayer. I say 'constant,' for the perfection of prayer does not lie within our power; as the Apostle Paul says, '*For we know not what we should pray for as we ought*' (Rom. viii, 26). Consequently it is just to pray often, to pray always, which falls within our power as the means of attaining purity of prayer, which is the mother of all spiritual blessings. 'Capture the Mother, and she will bring you the children,' said St. Isaac the Syrian. Learn first to acquire the power of prayer and you will easily practise all the other virtues. But those who know little of this form practical experience and the profoundest teaching of the holy Fathers, have no clear knowledge of it and speak of it but little."

During this talk, we had almost reached the monastery. And so as not to lose touch with this wise old man, and to get what I wanted more quickly, I hastened to say, "Be so kind, Reverend Father, as to show me what prayer without ceasing means and how it is learnt. I see you know all about these things."

He took my request kindly and asked me into his cell. "Come in," said he; "I will give you a volume of the holy Fathers from which with God's help you can learn about prayer clearly and in detail."

We went into his cell and he began to speak as follows. "The continuous interior Prayer of Jesus is a constant uninterrupted calling upon the divine Name of Jesus with the lips, in the spirit, in the heart; while forming a mental picture of His constant presence, and imploring His grace, during every occupation, at all times, in all places, even during sleep. The appeal is couched in these terms, 'Lord Jesus Christ, have mercy on me.' One who accustoms himself to this appeal experiences as a result so deep a consolation and so great a need to offer the prayer always, that he can no longer live without it, and it will continue to voice itself within him of its own accord. Now do you understand what prayer without ceasing is?"

"Yes indeed, Father, and in God's name teach me how to gain the habit of it," I cried, filled with joy.

"Read this book," he said. "It is called *The Philokalia*,[2] and it contains the full and detailed science of constant interior prayer, set forth by twenty-five holy Fathers. The book is marked by a lofty wisdom and is so profitable to use that it is considered the foremost and best manual of the contemplative spiritual life. As the revered Nicephorus said, 'It leads one to salvation without labour and sweat.' "

"Is it then more sublime and holy than the Bible?" I asked.

"No, it is not that. But it contains clear explanations of what the Bible holds in secret and which cannot be easily grasped by our short-sighted understanding. I will give you an illustration. The sun is the greatest, the most resplendent and the most wonderful of heavenly luminaries, but you cannot contemplate and examine it simply with unprotected eyes. You have to use a piece of artificial glass which is many millions of times smaller and darker than the sun. But through this little piece of glass you can examine the magnificent monarch of stars, delight in it, and endure its fiery rays. Holy Scripture also is a dazzling sun, and this book, *The Philokalia*, is the piece of glass which we use to enable us to contemplate the sun in its imperial splendour. Listen now, I am going to read you the sort of instruction it gives on unceasing interior prayer."

He opened the book, found the instruction by St. Simeon the New Theologian, and read: "Sit down alone and in silence. Lower your head, shut your eyes, breathe out gently and imagine yourself looking into your own

[2] *Philokalia* (in Russian: *Dobrotolyubie*). "The love of Spiritual Beauty." The title of the great collection of mystical and ascetic writings by Fathers of the Eastern Orthodox Church, over a period of eleven centuries.

heart. Carry your mind, *i.e.,* your thoughts, from your head to your heart. As you breathe out, say 'Lord Jesus Christ, have mercy on me.' Say it moving your lips gently, or simply say it in your mind. Try to put all other thoughts aside. Be calm, be patient, and repeat the process very frequently."

The old man explained all this to me and illustrated its meaning. We went on reading from *The Philokalia* passages of St. Gregory of Sinai, St. Callistus and St. Ignatius, and what we read from the book the *starets* explained in his own words. I listened closely and with great delight, fixed it in my memory, and tried as far as possible to remember every detail. In this way we spent the whole night together and went to Mattins without having slept at all.

The *starets* sent me away with his blessing and told me that while learning the Prayer I must always come back to him and tell him everything, making a very frank confession and report; for the inward process could not go on properly and successfully without the guidance of a teacher.

In church I felt a glowing eagerness to take all the pains I could to learn unceasing interior prayer, and I prayed to God to come to my help. Then I began to wonder how I should manage to see my *starets* again for counsel or confession, since leave was not given to remain for more than three days in the monastery guest-house, and there were no houses near.

However, I learned that there was a village between two and three miles from the monastery. I went there to look for a place to live, and to my great happiness God showed me the thing I needed. A peasant hired me for the whole summer to look after his kitchen garden, and what is more gave me the use of a little thatched hut in it where I could live alone. God be praised! I had found a quiet place. And in this manner I took up my abode and began to learn interior prayer in the way I had been shown, and to go to see my *starets* from time to time.

For a week, alone in my garden, I steadily set myself to learn to pray without ceasing exactly as the *starets* had explained. At first things seemed to go very well. But then it tired me very much. I felt lazy and bored and overwhelmingly sleepy, and a cloud of all sorts of other thoughts closed round me. I went in distress to my *starets* and told him the state I was in.

He greeted me in a friendly way and said, "My dear brother, it is the attack of the world of darkness upon you. To that world, nothing is worse than heartfelt prayer on our part. And it is trying by every means to hinder you and to turn you aside from learning the Prayer. But all the same the enemy only does what God sees fit to allow, and no more than is necessary for us. It would appear that you need a further testing of your humility, and that it is too soon, therefore, for your unmeasured zeal to approach the loftiest entrance to the heart. You might fall into spiritual covetousness. I will read you a little instruction from *The Philokalia* upon such cases."

He turned to the teaching of Nicephorus and read, " 'If after a few attempts you do not succeed in reaching the realm of your heart in the way you have been taught, do what I am about to say, and by God's help you will find what you seek. The faculty of pronouncing words lies in the throat. Reject all other thoughts (you can do this if you will) and allow that faculty to repeat only the following words constantly, "Lord Jesus Christ, have mercy on me." Compel yourself to do it always. If you succeed for a time, then without a doubt your heart also will open to prayer. We know it from experience.'

"There you have the teaching of the holy Fathers on such cases," said my *starets,* "and therefore you ought from today onwards to carry out my directions with confidence, and repeat the Prayer of Jesus as often as possible. Here is a rosary. Take it, and to start with say the Prayer three thousand times a day. Whether you are standing or sitting, walking or lying down, continually repeat 'Lord Jesus Christ, have mercy on me.' Say it quietly and without hurry, but without fail exactly three thousand times a day without deliberately increasing or diminishing the number. God will help you and by this means you will reach also the unceasing activity of the heart."

I gladly accepted this guidance and went home and began to carry out faithfully and exactly what my *starets* had bidden. For two days I found it rather difficult, but after that it became so easy and likeable, that as soon as I stopped, I felt a sort of need to go on saying the Prayer of Jesus, and I did it freely and willingly, not forcing myself to it as before.

I reported to my *starets,* and he bade me say the Prayer six thousand times a day, saying, "Be calm, just try as faithfully as possible to carry out the set number of prayers. God will vouchsafe you His grace."

In my lonely hut I said the Prayer of Jesus six thousand times a day for a whole week. I felt no anxiety. Taking no notice of any other thoughts however much they assailed me, I had but one object, *i.e.,* to carry out my *starets'* bidding exactly. And what happened? I grew so used to my Prayer that when I stopped for a single moment, I felt, so to speak, as though something were missing, as though I had lost something. The very moment I started the Prayer again, it went on easily and joyously. If I met anyone I had no wish to talk to him. All I wanted was to be alone and to say my Prayer, so used to it had I become in a week.

My *starets* had not seen me for ten days. On the eleventh day he came to see me himself, and I told him how things were going. He listened and said, "Now you have got used to the Prayer. See that you preserve the habit and strengthen it. Waste no time, therefore, but make up your mind by God's help from today to say the Prayer of Jesus twelve thousand times a day. Remain in your solitude, get up early, go to bed late, and come and ask advice of me every fortnight."

I did as he bade me. The first day I scarcely succeeded in finishing my task of saying twelve thousand prayers by late evening. The second day I did it easily and contentedly. To begin with, this ceaseless saying of the Prayer brought a certain amount of weariness, my tongue felt numbed, I had a stiff sort of feeling in my jaws, I had a feeling at first pleasant but afterwards slightly painful in the roof of my mouth. The thumb of my left hand, with which I counted my beads, hurt a little. I felt a slight inflammation in the whole of that wrist, and even up to the elbow, which was not unpleasant. Moreover, all this aroused me, as it were, and urged me on to frequent saying of the Prayer. For five days I did my set number of twelve thousand prayers, and as I formed the habit I found at the same time pleasure and satisfaction in it.

Early one morning the Prayer woke me up as it were. I started to say my usual morning prayers, but my tongue refused to say them easily or exactly. My whole desire was fixed upon one thing only—to say the Prayer of Jesus, and as soon as I went on with it I was filled with joy and relief. It was as though my lips and my tongue pronounced the words entirely of themselves without any urging from me. I spent the whole day in a state of the greatest contentment, I felt as though I was cut off from everything else. I lived as though in another world, and I easily finished my twelve thousand prayers by the early evening. I felt very much like still going on with them, but I did not dare to go beyond the number my *starets* had set me. Every day following I went on in the same way with my calling on the Name of Jesus Christ, and that with great readiness and liking. Then I went to see my *starets* and told him everything frankly and in detail.

He heard me out and then said, "Be thankful to God that this desire for the Prayer and this facility in it have been manifested in you. It is a natural consequence which follows constant effort and spiritual achievement. So a machine to the principal wheel of which one gives a drive, works for a long while afterwards by itself; but if it is to go on working still longer, one must oil it and give it another drive. Now you see with what admirable gifts God in His love for mankind has endowed even the bodily nature of man. You see what feelings can be produced even outside a state of grace in a soul which is sinful and with passions unsubdued, as you yourself have experienced. But how wonderful, how delightful and how consoling a thing it is when God is pleased to grant the gift of self-acting spiritual prayer, and to cleanse the soul from all sensuality! It is a condition which is impossible to describe, and the discovery of this mystery of prayer is a foretaste on earth of the bliss of Heaven. Such happiness is reserved for those who seek after God in the simplicity of a loving heart. Now I give you my permission to say your Prayer as often as you wish and as often as you can. Try to devote every moment you are awake to the Prayer, call on the Name of Jesus Christ without counting the number of times, and submit yourself humbly to the will of God, looking to Him for help. I am sure He will not forsake you, and that He will lead you into the right path."

Under this guidance I spent the whole summer in ceaseless oral prayer to Jesus Christ, and I felt absolute peace in my soul. During sleep I often dreamed that I was saying the Prayer. And during the day if I happened to meet anyone, all men without exception were as dear to me as if they had been my nearest relations. But I did not concern myself with them much. All my ideas were quite calmed of their own accord. I thought of nothing whatever but my Prayer, my mind tended to listen to it, and my heart began of itself to feel at times a certain warmth and pleasure. If I happened to go to church the lengthy service of the monastery seemed short to me, and no longer wearied me as it had in time past. My lonely hut seemed like a splendid palace, and I knew not how to thank God for having sent to me, a lost sinner, so wholesome a guide and master.

But I was not long to enjoy the teaching of my dear *starets,* who was so full of divine wisdom. He died at the end of the summer. Weeping freely I bade him farewell, and thanked him for the fatherly teaching he had given my wretched self, and as a blessing and a keepsake I begged for the rosary with which he said his prayers.

And so I was left alone. Summer came to an end and the kitchen garden was cleared. I had no longer anywhere to live. My peasant sent me away, giving me by way of wages two roubles, and filling up my bag with dried bread for my journey. Again I started off on my wanderings. But now I did not walk along as before, filled with care. The calling upon the Name of Jesus Christ gladdened my way. Everybody was kind to me, it was as though everyone loved me.

Then it occurred to me to wonder what I was to do with the money I had earned by my care of the kitchen garden. What good was it to me? Yet stay! I no longer had a *starets,* there was no one to go on teaching me.

Why not buy *The Philokalia* and continue to learn from it more about interior prayer?

I crossed myself and set off with my Prayer. I came to a large town, where I asked for the book in all the shops. In the end I found it, but they asked me three roubles for it, and I had only two. I bargained for a long time, but the shopkeeper would not budge an inch. Finally he said, "Go to this church near by, and speak to the churchwarden. He has a book like that, but it's a very old copy. Perhaps he will let you have it for two roubles." I went, and sure enough I found and bought for my two roubles a worn and old copy of *The Philokalia*. I was delighted with it. I mended my book as much as I could, I made a cover for it with a piece of cloth, and put it into my breast pocket with my Bible.

And that is how I go about now, and ceaselessly repeat the Prayer of Jesus, which is more precious and sweet to me than anything in the world. At times I do as much as forty-three or four miles a day, and do not feel that I am walking at all. I am aware only of the fact that I am saying my Prayer. When the bitter cold pierces me, I begin to say my Prayer more earnestly and I quickly get warm all over. When hunger begins to overcome me, I call more often on the Name of Jesus, and I forget my wish for food. When I fall ill and get rheumatism in my back and legs, I fix my thoughts on the Prayer and do not notice the pain. If anyone harms me I have only to think, "How sweet is the Prayer of Jesus!" and the injury and the anger alike pass away and I forget it all. I have become a sort of half-conscious person. I have no cares and no interests. The fussy business of the world I would not give a glance to. The one thing I wish for is to be alone, and all by myself to pray, to pray without ceasing; and doing this, I am filled with joy. God knows what is happening to me! Of course, all this is sensuous, or as my departed *starets* said, an artificial state which follows naturally upon routine. But because of my unworthiness and stupidity I dare not venture yet to go on further, and learn and make my own, spiritual prayer within the depths of my heart. I await God's time. And in the meanwhile I rest my hope on the prayers of my departed *starets*. Thus, although I have not yet reached that ceaseless spiritual prayer which is self-acting in the heart, yet I thank God I do now understand the meaning of those words I heard in the Epistle—*"Pray without ceasing."*

2

I WANDERED about for a long time in different districts, having for my fellow-traveller the Prayer of Jesus, which heartened and consoled me in all my journeys, in all my meetings with other people and in all the happenings of travel.

But I came to feel at last that it would be better for me to stay in some one place, in order to be alone more often, so as to be able to keep by myself and study *The Philokalia*. Although I read it whenever I found shelter for the night or rested during the day, yet I greatly wished to go more and more deeply into it, and with faith and heartfelt prayer to learn from it teaching about the truth for the salvation of my soul.

However, in spite of all my wishes, I could nowhere find any work that I was able to do, for I had lost the use of my left arm when quite a child. Seeing that because of this I should not be able to get myself a fixed abode, I made up my mind to go into Siberia to the tomb of St. Innocent of Irkutsk. My idea was that in the forests and steppes of Siberia I should travel in greater silence and therefore in a way that was better for prayer and reading. And this journey I undertook, all the while saying my oral Prayer without stopping.

After no great lapse of time I had the feeling that the Prayer had, so to speak, by its own action passed from my lips to my heart. That is to say, it seemed as though my heart in its ordinary beating began to say the words of the Prayer within at each beat. Thus for example, *one,* "Lord," *two,* "Jesus," *three,* "Christ," and so on. I gave up saying the Prayer with my lips. I simply listened carefully to what my heart was saying. It seemed as though my eyes looked right down into it; and I dwelt upon the words of my departed *starets* when he was telling me about this joy. Then I felt something like a slight pain in my heart, and in my thoughts so great a love for Jesus Christ that I pictured myself, if only I could see Him, throwing myself at His feet and not letting them go from my embrace, kissing them tenderly, and thanking Him with tears for having of His love and grace allowed me to find so great a consolation in His Name, me, His unworthy and sinful creature! Further there came into my heart a gracious warmth which spread through my whole breast. This moved me to a still closer reading of *The Philokalia* in order to test my feelings, and to make a thorough study of the business of secret prayer in the heart. For without such testing I was afraid of falling a victim to the mere charm of it, or of taking natural effects for the effects of grace, and of giving way to pride at my quick learning of the Prayer. It was of this danger that I had heard my departed *starets* speak. For this reason I took to walking more by night, and chose to spend my days reading *The Philokalia* sitting down under a tree in the forest. Ah! what wisdom, such as I had never known before, was shown me by this reading! Giving myself up to it I felt a delight which till then I had never been able to imagine. It is true that many places were still beyond the grasp of my dull mind. But my prayer in the heart brought with it the clearing up of things I did not understand. Sometimes also, though very rarely, I saw my departed *starets* in a dream, and he threw light upon many things, and, most of all, guided my ignorant soul more and more towards humility.

In this blissful state I passed more than two months of the summer. For the most part I went through the forests and along by-paths. When I came to a village I asked only for a bag of dried bread and a handful of salt. I filled my bark jar with water, and so on for another sixty miles or so.

Towards the end of the summer temptation began to attack me, perhaps as a result of the sins on my wretched soul, perhaps as something needed in the spiritual life, perhaps as the best way of giving me teaching and experience. A clear case in point was the following. One day when I came out on to the main road as twilight was falling, two men with shaved heads who looked like a couple of soldiers, came up to me. They demanded money. When I told them that I had not a farthing on me, they would not believe me, and shouted insolently, "You're lying, pilgrims always pick up lots of money."

"What's the good of arguing with him!" said one of them, and gave me such a blow on the head with his oak cudgel that I dropped senseless. I do not know whether I remained senseless long, but when I came to I found myself lying in the forest by the roadside robbed. My knapsack had gone, all that was left of it were the cords from which it hung, which they had cut. Thank God they had not stolen my passport, which I carried in my old fur cap so as to be able to show it as quickly as possible on demand. I got up weeping bitterly, not so much on account of the pain in my head as for the loss of my books, the Bible and *The Philokalia,* which were in the stolen knapsack.

Day and night I did not cease to weep and lament. Where was it now, my Bible which I had always carried with me, and which I had always read from my youth onwards? Where was my *Philokalia,* from which I had gained so much teaching and consolation? Oh unhappy me, to have lost the first and last treasures of my life before having had my fill of them! It would have been better to be killed outright than to live without this spiritual food. For I should never be able to replace the books now.

For two days I just dragged myself along, I was so crushed by the weight of my misfortune, and on the third I quite reached the end of my strength, and dropping down in the shelter of a bush I feel asleep. And then I had a dream. I was back at the monastery in the cell of my *starets* deploring my loss. The old man was trying to comfort me. He said, "Let this be a lesson to you in detachment from earthly things, for your better advance towards heaven. This has been allowed to happen to you to save you from falling into the mere enjoyment of spiritual things. God would have the Christian absolutely renounce all his desires and delights and attachments, and to submit himself entirely to His divine will. He orders every event for the help and salvation of

man; *He willeth that all men should be saved*. Take
courage then and believe that God *will with the temptation provide also a way of escape.* (1 Cor., x, 13.) Soon
you will be rejoicing much more than you are now distressed." At these words I awoke, feeling my strength
come back to me and my soul full of light and peace.
"God's will be done," I said. I crossed myself, got up
and went on my way. The Prayer again began to be active in my heart, as before, and for three days I went
along in peace.

All at once I came upon a body of convicts with their
military escort. When I came up to them I recognised
the two men who had robbed me. They were in the outside file, and so I fell at their feet and earnestly begged
them to tell me what they had done with my books. At
first they paid no heed to me, but in the end one of them
said, "If you will give us something we will tell you
where your books are. Give us a rouble." I swore to
them that even if I had to beg the rouble from someone
for the love of God, I would certainly give it to them,
and by way of pledge I offered them my passport. Then
they told me that my books were in the wagons which
followed the prisoners, among all the other stolen things
they were found with.

"How can I get them?"

"Ask the officer in charge of us."

I hurried to the officer and told him the whole story.

"Can you really read the Bible?" he asked me.

"Yes," I answered, "not only can I read everything,
but what is more, I can write too. You will see a signature in the Bible which shows it is mine, and here is my
passport showing the same name and surname."

He then told me that the rascals who had robbed me
were deserters living in a mud hut in the forest and that
they had plundered many people, but that a clever driver whose *troika* they had tried to steal had captured
them the day before. "All right," he added, "I will give
you your books back if they are there, but you come
with us as far as our halting place for the night; it is only
a little over two miles, then I need not stop the whole
convoy and the wagons just for your sake." I agreed to

this gladly, and as I walked along at his horse's side, we began to talk.

I saw that he was a kindly and honest fellow and no longer young. He asked me who I was, where I came from, and where I was going. I answered all his questions without hiding anything, and so we reached the house which marked the end of the day's march. He found my books and gave them back to me, saying, "Where are you going, now night has come on? Stay here and sleep in my ante-room." So I stayed.

Now that I had my books again, I was so glad that I did not know how to thank God. I clasped the books to my breast and held them there so long that my hands got quite numbed. I shed tears of joy, and my heart beat with delight. The officer watched me and said, "You must love reading your Bible very much!" But such was my joy that I could not answer him, I could only weep. Then he went on to say, "I also read the Gospel regularly every day, brother." He produced a small copy of the Gospels, printed in Kiev and bound in silver, saying, "Sit down, and I will tell you how it came about."

"Hullo there, let us have some supper," he shouted.

We drew up to the table and the officer began his story.

"Ever since I was a young man I have been with the army in the field and not on garrison service. I knew my job, and my superior officers liked me for a conscientious second-lieutenant. Still, I was young, and so were my friends. Unhappily I took to drink, and drunkenness became a regular passion with me. So long as I kept away from drink, I was a good officer, but when I gave way to it, I was no good for anything for six weeks at a time. They bore with me for a long while, but the end of it was that after being thoroughly rude while drunk to my commanding officer, I was cashiered and transferred to a garrison as a private soldier for three years. I was threatened with a still more severe punishment if I did not give up drinking and mend my ways. Even in this miserable state of affairs, however much I tried, I could not regain my self-control, nor cure myself. I found it impossible to get rid of my passion for drink, and it was decided to send me to a disciplinary corps. When I was informed of this I was at my wits' end. I was in barracks occupied with my wretched thoughts when there arrived a monk who was going round collecting for a church. We each of us gave him what we could.

"He came up to me and asked me why I was so unhappy, and I talked to him and told him my troubles. He sympathised with me and said, 'The same thing happened to my own brother, and what do you think helped him? His spiritual father gave him a copy of the Gospels with strict orders to read a chapter without a moment's delay every time he felt a longing for wine coming over him. If the desire continued he was to read a second chapter, and so on. That is what my brother did, and at the end of a very short time his drunkenness came to an end. It is now fifteen years since he touched a drop of alcohol. You do the same and you will see how that will help you. I have a copy of the Gospels which you must let me bring you.'

"I listened to him, and then I said, 'How can your Gospels help me since all efforts of my own and all the medical treatment have failed to stop me drinking?' I talked in that way because I had as yet never been in the habit of reading the Gospels. 'Don't say that,' replied the monk, 'I assure you that it will be a help.' As a matter of fact, the next day he brought me this very copy. I opened it, took a glance, and said, 'I cannot accept it, I am not used to Church Slavonic and don't understand it.' But the monk went on to assure me that in the very words of the Gospel there lay a gracious power, for in them was written what God Himself had spoken. 'It does not matter very much if at first you do not understand, go on reading diligently. A monk once said, "If you do not understand the Word of God, the devils understand what you are reading, and tremble," and your drunkenness is certainly the work of devils. And here is another thing I will tell you. St. John Chrysostom writes that even a room in which a copy of the Gospels is kept, holds the spirits of darkness at bay, and becomes an unpromising field for their wiles.'

"I forget what I gave the monk. But I bought his book of the Gospels, put it away in a trunk with my other things and forgot it. Some while afterwards a bout of drunkenness threatened me. An irresistible desire for drink drove me hurriedly to open my trunk to get some money and rush off to the public-house. But the first thing my eyes fell on was the copy of the Gospels, and all that the monk had said came back vividly to my mind. I opened the book and began to read the first chapter of St. Matthew. I got to the end of it without understanding a word. Still I remembered that the monk had said, 'No matter if you do not understand, go on reading diligently.' 'Come,' said I, 'I must read the second chapter.' I did so and began to understand a little. So I started on the third chapter and then the barracks bell began to ring; everyone had to go to bed, no one was allowed to go out, and I had to stay where I was. When I got up in the morning I was just on the point of going out to get some wine when I suddenly thought— supposing I were to read another chapter? What would be the result? I read it and I did not go to the public-house. Again I felt the craving, and again I read a chapter. I felt a certain amount of relief. This encouraged me, and from that time on, whenever I felt the need of a drink, I used to read a chapter of the Gospels. What is more, as time went on things got better and better, and by the time I had finished all four Gospels my drunkenness was absolutely a thing of the past, and I felt nothing but disgust for it. It is just twenty years now since I drank a drop of alcohol.

"Everybody was astonished at the change brought about in me. Some three years later my commission was restored to me. In due course I was promoted, and finally got my majority. I married; I am blessed with a good wife, we have made a position for ourselves, and so, thank God, we go on living our life. As far as we can, we help the poor and give hospitality to pilgrims. Why, now I have a son who is an officer and a first-rate fellow. And mark this—since the time when I was cured of drunkenness, I have lived under a vow to read the Gospels every single day of my life, one whole Gospel in every twenty-four hours, and I let nothing whatever hinder me. I do this still. If I am exceedingly pressed with business, and unusually tired, I lie down and get my wife or my son to read the whole of one of the Evangelists to me, and so avoid breaking my rule. By way of thanksgiving and for the glory of God I have had this book of the Gospels mounted in pure silver, and I always carry it in my breast pocket."

I listened with great joy to this story of his. "I also have come across a case of the same sort," I told him. "At the factory in our village there was a craftsman, very skilful at his job, and a good, kindly fellow. Unhappily, however, he also drank, and very often at that. A certain God-fearing man advised him when the desire for drink seized him, to repeat the Prayer of Jesus thirty-three times in honour of the Holy Trinity, and in memory of the thirty-three years of the earthly life of Jesus Christ. He took his advice and started to carry it out, and very soon he quite gave up drinking. And, what is more, three years later he went into a monastery."

"And which is the best," he asked, "the Prayer of Jesus, or the Gospels?"

"It's all one and the same thing," I answered. "What the Gospel is, that the Prayer of Jesus is also, for the Divine Name of Jesus Christ holds in itself the whole gospel truth. The holy Fathers say that the Prayer of Jesus is a summary of the Gospels."

After our talk we said prayers, and the Major began to read the Gospel of St. Mark from the beginning, and I listened and said the Prayer in my heart. At two o'clock in the morning he came to the end of the Gospel, and we parted and went to bed.

As usual I got up early in the morning. Everyone was still asleep. As soon as it began to get light, I eagerly seized my beloved *Philokalia*. With what gladness I opened it! I might have been getting a glimpse of my own father coming back from a far country, or of a friend risen from the dead. I kissed it, and thanked God for giving it me back again. I began at once to read Theolept of Philadelphia, in the second part of the book. His teaching surprised me when he lays down that one and the same person at one and the same time should do three quite different things. "Seated at table," he says, "supply your body with food, your ear with reading and your mind with prayer." But the memory of the very happy evening the day before really gave me from my own experience the meaning of this thought. And here also the secret was revealed to me that the mind and the heart are not one and the same thing.

As soon as the Major rose I went to thank him for his kindness and to say good-bye. He gave me tea and a rouble and bade me farewell. I set off again feeling very happy. I had gone over half a mile when I remembered I had promised the soldiers a rouble, and that now this rouble had come to me in a quite unlooked-for way. Should I give it to them or not? At first I thought: they beat you and they robbed you, moreover this money will be of no use to them whatever, since they are under arrest. But afterwards other thoughts came to me. Remember it is written in the Bible, *"If thine enemy hunger feed him,"* and Jesus Christ himself said, *"Love your enemies," "And if any man will take away thy coat let him have thy cloak also."* That settled it for me. I went back and just as I got to the house all the convicts came out to start on the next stage of their march. I went quickly up to my two soldiers, I handed them my rouble and said, "Repent and pray! Jesus Christ loves men, He will not forsake you." And with that I left them and went on my way.

After doing some thirty miles along the main road I thought I would take a by-path so that I might be more by myself and read more quietly. For a long while I walked through the heart of the forest, and but rarely came upon a village. At times I passed almost the whole day sitting under the trees and carefully reading *The Philokalia,* from which I gained a surprising amount of knowledge. My heart kindled with desire for union with God by means of interior prayer, and I was eager to learn it under the guidance and control of my book. At the same time I felt sad that I had no dwelling where I could give myself up quietly to reading all the while. During this time I read my Bible also, and I felt that I began to understand it more clearly than before, when I had failed to understand many things in it and had often been a prey to doubts. The holy Fathers were right when they said that *The Philokalia* is a key to the mysteries of Holy Scripture. With the help it gave me I began to some extent to understand the hidden meaning of the Word of God. I began to see the meaning of such sayings as—"The inner secret man of the heart," "true prayer worships in the spirit," "the kingdom is within us," "the intercession of the Holy Spirit with groanings that cannot be uttered," "abide in me," "give me thy heart," "to put on Christ," "the betrothal of the Spirit to our hearts," the cry from the depths of the heart, "Abba, Father," and so on. And when with all this in mind I prayed with my heart, everything around me seemed delightful and marvellous. The trees, the grass, the birds, the earth, the air, the light seemed to be telling me that they existed for man's sake, that they witnessed to the love of God for man, that everything proved the love of God for man, that all things prayed to God and sang His praise.

Thus it was that I came to understand what *The Philokalia* calls "the knowledge of the speech of all creatures," and I saw the means by which converse could be held with God's creatures.

In this way I wandered about for a long while, coming at length to so lonely a district that for three days I came upon no village at all. My supply of dried bread was used up, and I began to be very much cast down at the thought I might die of hunger. I began to pray my hardest in the depths of my heart. All my fears went, and I entrusted myself to the will of God. My peace of mind came back to me, and I was in good spirits again. When I had gone a little further along the road, which here skirted a huge forest, I caught sight of a dog which came out of it and ran along in front of me. I called it, and it came up to me with a great show of friendliness. I was glad, and I thought, Here is another case of God's goodness! No doubt there is a flock grazing in the forest and this dog belongs to the shepherd. Or perhaps somebody is shooting in the neighbourhood. Whichever it is I shall be able to beg a piece of bread if nothing more, for I have eaten nothing for twenty-four hours. Or at least I shall be able to find out where the nearest village is.

After jumping around me for some little time and seeing that I was not going to give him anything, the dog trotted back into the forest along the narrow footpath by which he had come out. I followed, and a few hundred yards further on, looking between the trees, I saw him run into a hole, from which he looked out and began to bark. At the same time a thin and pale middle-aged peasant came into view from behind a great tree. He asked me where I came from, and for my part I wanted to know how he came to be there, and so we started a friendly talk.

He took me into his mud hut and told me that he was a forester and that he looked after this particular wood, which had been sold for felling. He set bread and salt before me, and we began to talk. "How I envy you," said I, "being able to live so nicely alone in this quiet instead of being like me! I wander from place to place and rub along with all sorts of people."

"You can stop here too, if you like," he answered. "The old forester's hut is quite near here. It is half ruined, but still quite fit to live in in summer. I suppose you have your passport. As far as bread goes, we shall always have plenty of that, it is brought to me every week from my village. This spring here never dries up. For my part, brother, I have eaten nothing but bread and have drunk nothing but water for the last ten years. This is how things stand. When autumn comes and the peasants have ended their work on the land, some two hundred workmen will be coming to cut down this wood. Then I shall have no further business here, and you will not be allowed to stay either."

As I listened to all this I all but fell at his feet, I felt so pleased. I did not know how to thank God for such goodness. In this unlooked-for way my greatest wish was to be granted me. There were still over four months before next autumn; during all that time I could enjoy the silence and peace needed for a close reading of *The Philokalia* in order to study and learn ceaseless prayer in the heart. So I very gladly stayed there, to live during that time in the hut he showed me.

I talked further with this simple brother who gave me shelter, and he told me about his life and his ideas. "I had quite a good position in the life of our village," said he. "I had a workshop where I dyed fustian and linen, and I lived comfortably enough, though not without sin.

I often cheated in business, I was a false swearer, I was abusive, I used to drink and quarrel. In our village there was an old *dyachok*[3] who had a very old book on the Last Judgment. He used to go from house to house and read from it, and he was paid something for doing so. He came to me too. Give him threepence and a glass of wine into the bargain and he would go on reading all night till cock crow. There I would sit at my work and listen while he read about the torments that await us in Hell. I heard how the living will be changed and the dead raised; how God will come down to judge the world; how the angels will sound the trumpets; I heard of the fire and pitch, and of the worm which will devour sinners. One day as I listened I was seized with horror, and I said to myself: What if these torments come upon me! I will set to work to save my soul. It may be that by prayer I can avoid the results of my sins. I thought about this for a long time. Then I gave up my work, sold my house, and as I was alone in the world, I got a place as forester here and all I ask of my *mir*[4] is bread, clothes and some candles for my prayers. I have been living like this for over ten years now. I eat only once a day and then nothing but bread and water. I get up at cock crow, make my devotions and say my prayers before the holy icons with seven candles burning. When I make my rounds in the forest during the day, I wear iron chains weighing sixty pounds next to my skin. I never grumble, drink neither wine nor beer, I never quarrel with anybody at all, and I have had nothing to do with women and girls all my life. At first this sort of life pleased me, but lately other thoughts have come into my mind, and I cannot get away from them. God only knows if I shall be able to pray my sins away in this

[3] *Dyachok.* A minister whose chief liturgical function is to chant psalms and the Epistle in the Russian Church.

[4] *Mir.* The Assembly of all the peasant householders in a village. It was a very ancient institution, in which the peasants only had a voice, even the great landowners being excluded. The *mir* enjoyed a certain measure of self-government, and elected representatives to the larger peasant assembly of the *volost*, which included several *mirs*. The *starosta* was the elected headman of the *mir*.

fashion, and it's a hard life. And is everything written in that book true? How can a dead man rise again? Supposing he has been dead over a hundred years and not even his ashes are left? Who knows if there is really a Hell or not? What more is known of a man after he dies and rots? Perhaps the book was written by priests and masters to make us poor fools afraid and keep us quiet. What if we plague ourselves for nothing and give up all our pleasure in vain? Suppose there is no such thing as another life, what then? Isn't it better to enjoy one's earthly life, and take it easily and happily? Ideas of this kind often worry me, and I don't know but what I shall not some day go back to my old work."

I heard him with pity. They say, I thought, that it is only the learned and the clever who are free thinkers and believe in nothing! Yet here is one of ourselves, even a simple peasant, a prey to such unbelief. The kingdom of darkness throws open its gates to everyone, it seems, and maybe attacks the simple-minded most easily. Therefore one must learn wisdom and strengthen oneself with the Word of God as much as possible against the enemy of the soul.

So with the object of helping this brother and doing all I could to strengthen his faith, I took *The Philokalia* out of my knapsack. Turning to the 109th chapter of Isikhi, I read it to him. I set out to prove to him the uselessness and vanity of avoiding sin merely from fear of the tortures of Hell, I told him that the soul could be freed from sinful thoughts only by guarding the mind and cleansing the heart, and that this could be done by interior prayer. I added that according to the holy Fathers, one who performs saving works simply from the fear of Hell follows the way of bondage, and he who does the same just in order to be rewarded with the Kingdom of Heaven follows the path of a bargainer with God. The one they call a slave, the other a hireling. But God wants us to come to Him as sons to their Father, He wants us to behave ourselves honourably from love for Him and zeal for His service, He wants us to find our happiness in uniting ourselves with Him in a saving union of mind and heart.

"However much you spend yourself on treating your

body hardly," I said, "you will never find peace of mind that way, and unless you have God in your mind and the ceaseless Prayer of Jesus in your heart, you will always be likely to fall back into sin for the very slightest reason. Set to work, my brother, upon the ceaseless saying of the Prayer of Jesus. You have such a good chance of doing so here in this lonely place, and in a short while you will see the gain of it. No godless thoughts will then be able to get at you, and the true faith and love for Jesus Christ will be shown to you. You will then understand how the dead will be raised, and you will see the Last Judgment in its true light. The Prayer will make you feel such lightness and such bliss in your heart, that you will be astonished at it yourself, and your wholesome way of life will be neither dull nor troublesome to you."

Then I went on to explain to him as well as I could how to begin, and how to go on ceaselessly with the Prayer of Jesus, and how the Word of God and the writings of the holy Fathers teach us about it. He agreed with it all and seemed to me to be calmer.

Then I left him and shut myself up in the hut which he had shown me. Ah! how delighted I was, how calmly happy when I crossed the threshold of that lonely retreat, or rather, that tomb! It seemed to me like a magnificent palace filled with every consolation and delight. With tears of rapture I gave thanks to God and said to myself, "Here in this peace and quietude I must seriously set to work at my task and beseech God to give me light." So I started by reading through *The Philokalia* again with great care, from beginning to end. Before long I had read the whole of it, and I saw how much wisdom, holiness and depth of insight there was in this book. Still, so many matters were dealt with in it, and it contained such a lot of lessons from the holy Fathers, that I could not very well grasp it all, and take in as a single whole what was said about interior prayer. And this was what I chiefly wanted to know, so as to learn from it how to practise ceaseless self-acting prayer in the heart.

This was my great desire, following the divine command in the Apostle's words, "*Covet earnestly the best gifts,*" and again, "*Quench not the Spirit.*" I thought over the matter for a long time. What was to be done? My mind and my understanding were not equal to the task, and there was no one to explain. I made up my mind to besiege God with prayer. Maybe He would make me understand somehow. For twenty-four hours I did nothing but pray without stopping for a single moment. At last my thoughts were calmed, and I fell asleep. And then I dreamed that I was in my departed *starets'* cell and that he was explaining *The Philokalia* to me. "The holy book is full of profound wisdom," he was saying. "It is a secret treasury of the meaning of the hidden judgments of God. It is not everywhere and to everyone that it is accessible, but it does give to each such guidance as he needs, to the wise, wise guidance, to the simple-minded, simple guidance. That is why you simple folk should not read the chapters one after the other as they are arranged in the book. That order is for those who are instructed in theology. Those who are uninstructed, but who nevertheless desire to learn interior prayer from this book, should take things in this order. (1) First of all read through the book of Nicephorus the monk (in part 2), then (2) the whole book of Gregory of Sinai, except the short chapters, (3) Simeon the New Theologian on the Three Forms of Prayer and his discourse on Faith, and after that (4) the book of Callistus and Ignatius. In these Fathers there are full directions and teaching on interior prayer of the heart, in a form which everyone can understand.

"And if, in addition, you want to find a very understandable instruction on prayer, turn to part 4 and find the summarised pattern of prayer by the most holy Callistus, Patriarch of Constantinople."

In my dream I held the book in my hands and began to look for this passage, but I was quite unable to find it. Then he turned over a few pages himself and said, "Here it is, I will mark it for you." He picked up a piece of charcoal from the ground and made a mark in the margin, against the passage he had found. I listened to him with care, and tried to fix in my mind everything he said, word for word. When I woke up it was still dark. I lay still and in thought went over my dream and all that my *starets* had said to me. "God knows," thought I, "whether it is really the spirit of my departed *starets* that I have seen, or whether it is only the outcome of my own thoughts, because they are so often taken up with *The Philokalia* and my *starets*." With this doubt in my mind I got up, for day was beginning to break; and what did I see? There on the stone which served as a table in my hut lay the book open at the very page which my *starets* had pointed out to me, and in the margin, a charcoal mark just as in my dream! Even the piece of charcoal itself was lying beside the book! I looked in astonishment, for I remembered clearly that the book was not there the evening before, that it had been put, shut, under my pillow, and also I was quite certain that before there had been nothing where now I saw the charcoal mark.

It was this which made me sure of the truth of my dream, and that my revered master of blessed memory was pleasing to God. I set about reading *The Philokalia* in the exact order he had bidden. I read it once, and again a second time, and this reading kindled in my soul a zealous desire to make what I had read a matter of practical experience. I saw clearly what interior prayer means, how it is to be reached, what the fruits of it are, how it filled one's heart and soul with delight, and how one could tell whether that delight came from God, from nature or from temptation.

So I began by searching out my heart in the way Simeon the New Theologian teaches. With my eyes shut I gazed in thought, *i.e.,* in imagination, upon my heart. I tried to picture it there in the left side of my breast and to listen carefully to its beating. I started doing this several times a day, for half an hour at a time, and at first I felt nothing but a sense of darkness. But little by little after a fairly short time I was able to picture my heart and to note its movement, and further with the help of my breathing I could put into it and draw from it the Prayer of Jesus in the manner taught by the saints, Gregory of Sinai, Callistus and Ignatius. When drawing the air in I looked in spirit into my heart and said, "Lord Jesus Christ," and when breathing out again, I said, "Have mercy on me." I did this at first for an hour at a time, then for two hours, then for as long as I could, and in the end almost all day long. If any difficulty arose, if sloth or doubt came upon me, I hastened to take up *The Philokalia* and read again those parts which dealt with the work of the heart, and then once more I felt ardour and zeal for the Prayer.

When about three weeks had passed I felt a pain in my heart, and then a most delightful warmth, as well as consolation and peace. This aroused me still more and spurred me on more and more to give great care to the saying of the Prayer so that all my thoughts were taken up with it and I felt a very great joy. From this time I began to have from time to time a number of different feelings in my heart and mind. Sometimes my heart would feel as though it were bubbling with joy, such lightness, freedom and consolation were in it. Sometimes I felt a burning love for Jesus Christ and for all God's creatures. Sometimes my eyes brimmed over with tears of thankfulness to God, who was so merciful to me, a wretched sinner. Sometimes my understanding, which had been so stupid before, was given so much light that I could easily grasp and dwell upon matters of which up to now I had not been able even to think at all. Sometimes that sense of a warm gladness in my heart spread throughout my whole being and I was deeply moved as the fact of the presence of God everywhere was brought home to me. Sometimes by calling upon the Name of Jesus I was overwhelmed with bliss, and now I knew the meaning of the words "*The Kingdom of God is within you.*"

From having all these and other like feelings I noted that interior prayer bears fruit in three ways: in the Spirit, in the feelings, and in revelations. In the first, for instance, is the sweetness of the love of God, inward peace, gladness of mind, purity of thought, and the sweet remembrance of God. In the second, the pleasant warmth of the heart, fulness of delight in all one's limbs, the joyous "bubbling" in the heart, lightness and courage, the joy of living, power not to feel sickness and sorrow. And in the last, light given to the mind, understanding of Holy Scripture, knowledge of the speech of created things, freedom from fuss and vanity, knowledge of the joy of the inner life, and finally certainty of the nearness of God and His love for us.

After spending five months in this lonely life of prayer and such happiness as this, I grew so used to the Prayer that I went on with it all the time. In the end I felt it going on of its own accord within my mind and in the depths of my heart, without any urging on my part. Not only when I was awake, but even during sleep just the same thing went on. Nothing broke into it and it never stopped even for a single moment, whatever I might be doing. My soul was always giving thanks to God and my heart melted away with unceasing happiness.

The time came for the wood to be felled. People began to come along in crowds, and I had to leave my quiet dwelling. I thanked the forester, said some prayers, kissed the bit of the earth which God had deigned to give me, unworthy of His mercy as I was, shouldered my bag of books, and set off.

For a very long while I wandered about in different places until I reached Irkutsk. The self-acting Prayer in my heart was a comfort and consolation all the way; whatever I met with it never ceased to gladden me, though it did so to different degrees at different times. Wherever I was, whatever I did or gave myself up to, it never hindered things, nor was hindered by them. If I am working at anything the Prayer goes on by itself in my heart, and the work gets on faster. If I am listening carefully to anything, or reading, the Prayer never stops, at one and the same time I am aware of both just as if I were made into two people, or as if there were two souls in my one body. Lord! what a mysterious thing man is! *"How manifold are thy works, O Lord! In wisdom hast Thou made them all."*

All sorts of things and many strange adventures happened to me as I went on my way. If I were to start telling them all, I should not end in twenty-four hours. Thus for example, one winter evening as I was going alone through the forest towards a village which I could see about a mile away, and where I was to spend the night, a great wolf suddenly came in sight and made for me. I had in my hand my *starets'* woollen rosary, which

I always carried with me. I struck at the animal with that. Well, the rosary was torn out of my hands and got twisted round the wolf's neck. He leapt away from me, but in jumping through a thorn bush he got his hind paws caught. The rosary also caught on a bough of a dead tree and he began dashing himself about, but he could not free himself because the rosary was tightening round his throat. I crossed myself in faith and went forward to free him, chiefly because I was afraid that if he tore my rosary away and ran off with it, I should lose my precious rosary. And sure enough, as soon as I got hold of the rosary the wolf snapped it and fled without leaving a trace. I thanked God, with my blessed *starets* in mind, and I came safe and sound to the village, where I asked for a night's lodging at an inn.

I went into the house. Two men, one of them old and the other middle-aged and heavily built, were sitting at a table in a corner drinking tea. They looked as though they were not just simple folk, and I asked the peasant who was with their horses who they were. He told me that the elder of the two was a teacher at an elementary school, and the other the clerk of the County Court. They were both people of the better class. He was driving them to a fair about a dozen miles away. After sitting a while, I asked the hostess to lend me a needle and thread, came over into the candle-light, and set about mending my broken rosary.

The clerk watched what I was doing and said, "I suppose you have been praying so hard that your rosary broke?"

"It was not I who broke it," I answered, "it was a wolf."

"What! A wolf? Do wolves say their prayers, too?" said he jokingly.

I told them all that had happened, and how precious the rosary was to me. The clerk laughed again, saying, "Miracles are always happening with you sham saints! What was there sacred about a thing like that? The simple fact was that you brandished something at the wolf and he was frightened and went off. Of course, dogs and wolves take fright at the gesture of throwing, and getting caught on to a tree is common enough. That sort of thing very often happens. Where is the miracle?"

But the old man answered him thus: "Do not jump to conclusions like that, sir. You miss the deeper aspects of the incident. For my part I see in this peasant's story the mystery of nature, both sensuous and spiritual."

"How's that?" asked the clerk.

"Well, like this. Although you have not received the highest education, you have, of course, learned the sacred history of the Old and New Testaments, as summarised in the questions and answers used at school. You remember that when our father Adam was still in a state of holy innocence all the animals were obedient to him, they approached him in fear and received from him their names. The old man to whom this rosary belonged was a saint. Now what is the meaning of sanctity? For the sinner it means nothing else than a return through effort and discipline to the state of innocence of the first man. When the soul is made holy the body becomes holy also. The rosary had always been in the hands of a sanctified person; the effect of the contact of his hands and the exhalation of his body was to inoculate it with holy power—the power of the first man's innocence. That is the mystery of spiritual nature! All animals in natural succession down to the present time have experienced this power, and they experience it through smelling, for in all animals the nose is the chief organ of sensation. That is the mystery of sensuous nature!"

"You learned people go on about strength and wisdom," said the clerk, "but we take things more simply. Fill up a glass of vodka and tip it off; that will give you strength enough." And he went over to the cupboard.

"That's your business," said the schoolmaster, "but please leave learning to us!"

I liked the way he spoke, and I came up closer to him and said, "May I venture, Father, to tell you a little more about my *starets*?" And so I told him about the appearance of my *starets* while I was asleep, the teaching he had given me, and the charcoal mark which he had made in *The Philokalia*. He listened with care to what I told him, but the clerk, who lay stretched out on a bench, muttered, "It's true enough you can lose your wits through reading the Bible too much. That's what it is! Do you suppose a bogy man comes and marks your books at night? You simply let the book drop on the ground yourself while you were asleep, and some soot made a dirty mark on it. There's your miracle! Eh, you tricksters, I've come across plenty of your kidney!"

Muttering this sort of thing, the clerk rolled over with his face to the wall and went to sleep. So I turned to the schoolmaster, saying, "If I may, I will show you the actual book. Look, it is really marked, not just dirtied with soot." I took it out of my knapsack and showed him. "What surprises me," said I, "is how a spirit without a body could have picked up a piece of charcoal and written with it." He looked at the mark and said, "This also is a spiritual mystery. I will explain it to you. Look here now, when spirits appear in a bodily form to a living person, they compose themselves a body which can be felt, from the air and the worldstuff, and later on give back to the elements again what they had borrowed from them. Just as the atmosphere possesses elasticity, a power to contract and expand, so the soul, clothed in it, can take up anything, and act, and write. But what is this book of yours? Let me have a look at it." He began to look at it and it opened at the sermons of St. Simeon the New Theologian. "Ah, this must be a theological work. I have never seen it before," he said.

"It is almost wholly made up," I told him, "of teaching on interior prayer of the heart in the Name of Jesus Christ. It is set forth here in full detail by twenty-five holy Fathers."

"Ah, I know something of interior prayer," he answered.

I bowed before him, down to the very ground, and begged him to speak to me about interior prayer.

"Well, it says in the New Testament that man and all creation '*are subject to vanity, not willingly,*' and sigh with effort and desire to enter into the liberty of the children of God. The mysterious sighing of creation, the innate aspiration of every soul towards God, that is exactly what interior prayer is. There is no need to learn it, it is innate in every one of us!"

"But what is one to do to find it in oneself, to feel it

in one's heart, to acknowledge it by one's will, to take it and feel the happiness and light of it, and so to reach salvation?" I asked.

"I don't know whether there is anything on the subject in theological books," said he.

"Well, here it is. It is all explained here," I answered, showing him my book again. The schoolmaster noted the title and said he would certainly have one sent from Tobolsk and study it. After that we went our different ways. I thanked God for this talk with the schoolmaster, and prayed that God would so order things that the clerk also might read *The Philokalia*, even if only once, and let him find salvation through it.

Another time—it was in spring—I passed through a village where I stayed with the priest. He was a worthy man, living alone, and I spent three days with him. Having watched me for that length of time he said to me, "Stay here. I will pay you something. I need a trustworthy man; as you see, we are starting to build a stone church here near the old wooden chapel, and I have been looking for some honest person to keep an eye on the workmen and stay in the chapel in charge of the offerings for the building fund. It is exactly the thing for you, and would just suit your way of life. You will be alone in the chapel and say your prayers. There is a quiet little room for a verger there. Please stay, at any rate until the building is finished."

For a long while I refused, but in the end I had to yield to the good priest's begging, and I stayed there till the autumn, taking up my abode in the chapel. At first I found it quiet and apt for prayer, although a great many people came to the chapel, especially on holidays, some to say their prayers, some because they were bored, and others again with the idea of pilfering from the collection plate. I read my Bible and my *Philokalia* every evening, and some of them saw this and started talking to me about it or asked me to read aloud.

After a while I noticed that a young village girl often came to the chapel, and spent a long while in prayer. Listening to her whisperings, I found that the prayers she was saying were some of them strange to me, and others the usual prayers in a garbled form. I asked her where she learned such things, and she told me it was from her mother, who was a churchwoman, but that her father belonged to a sect which had no priesthood. Feeling sorry for her, I advised her to read her prayers in the right form as given by the tradition of Holy Church. Then I taught her the right wording of the Lord's Prayer and of the Hail Mary, and finally I advised her to say the Prayer of Jesus as often as she could, for that brought one nearer to God than any other prayer. The girl took note of what I said and set about it quite simply. And what happened? A short time afterwards she told me that she was so used to the Prayer that she felt it draw her all the time, that she used it as much as she could, that she enjoyed the Prayer at the time, and that afterwards she was filled with gladness and a wish to begin using it again. I was glad of this, and advised her to go on with it more and more.

Summer was drawing to a close. Many visitors to the chapel came to see me also, not only to be read to and to ask for advice, but with all sorts of worldly troubles, and even to ask about things they had mislaid or lost. Some of them seemed to take me for a wizard. The girl I spoke about also came to me one day in a state of great distress and worry, not knowing what to do. Her father wanted to make her marry a man of his own religion, and they were to be married not by a priest but by a mere peasant belonging to the same sect. "How could that be a lawful marriage, wouldn't it be the same thing as fornication?" cried the girl. She had made up her mind to run away somewhere or other.

"But," said I, "where to? They would be sure to find you again. They will look everywhere, and you won't be able to hide anywhere from them. You had better pray earnestly to God to turn your father from his purpose and to guard your soul from sin and heresy. That is a much sounder plan than running away."

Thus time passed away, and all this noise and fuss began to be more than I could bear, and at last at the end of summer I made up my mind to leave the chapel and go on with my pilgrimage as before. I told the priest what was in my mind, saying, "You know my plans, Father, I must have quiet for prayer, and here it is very disturbing and bad for me, and I have spent the whole summer here. Now let me go, and give your blessing on my lonely journey."

But the priest did not want to let me go, and tried to get me to stay. "What is there to hinder your praying here? Your work is nothing to speak of, beyond stopping in the chapel. You have your daily bread. Say your prayers then all day and all night if you like, and live with God. You are useful here, you don't go in for silly gossip with the people who come here, you are a source of profit to the church. All that is worth more in God's sight than your prayers all by yourself. Why do you always want to be alone? Common prayer is pleasanter. God did not create man to think of himself only, but that men should help each other and lead each other along the path to salvation, each according to his strength. Think of the saints and the Fathers of the Church! They bustled about day and night, they cared for the needs of the Church, they used to preach all over the place. They didn't sit down alone and hide themselves from people."

"Everyone has his own gift from God," I answered. "There have been many preachers, Father, but there have also been many hermits. Everyone does what he can, as he sees his own line, with the thought that God Himself shows him the way of his salvation. How do you get over the fact that many of the saints gave up their positions as bishops or priests or the rule of a monastery and went into the desert to get away from the fuss which comes from living with other people? St. Isaac the Syrian, for instance, fled from the flock whose bishop he was, and the venerable Athanasius of Athos left his large monastery just because to them these places were a source of temptation, and they sincerely believed Our Lord's saying, *'What shall it profit a man if he gains the whole world and lose his own soul?'* "

"Ah, but they were saints," said the priest.

"And if," I answered, "the very saints took steps to guard themselves from the dangers of mingling with people, what else, I ask you, can a feeble sinner do?"

So in the end I said good-bye to this good priest, and he, out of the love in his heart, set me on my way.

Some half-dozen miles further on, I stopped for the night at a village. At the inn there I found a peasant hopelessly ill, and I advised those who were with him to see that he had the last sacraments. They agreed, and towards morning sent for the parish priest. I stayed there too, because I wanted to worship and pray in the presence of the Holy Gifts, and going out into the street, sat down on the *zavalina*[5] to wait for the priest to come. All at once I was astonished to see running towards me from the backyard the girl who used to pray in the chapel.

"What brings you here?" I asked.

"They had fixed the day of my betrothal to the man I told you of, so I left them." And kneeling before me she went on, "Have pity on me: take me with you and put me into some convent or other. I don't want to be married, I want to live in a convent and say the Jesus Prayer. They will listen to you and take me."

"Goodness!" I exclaimed, "and where am I to take you to? I don't know a single convent in this neighbourhood. Besides, I can't take you anywhere without a passport. For one thing, you wouldn't be taken in anywhere, and for another it would be quite impossible for you to hide nowadays. You would be caught at once and sent home again, and punished as a tramp into the bargain. You had far better go home and say your prayers there. And if you don't want to marry, make out that you are ill. The holy mother Clementa did that, and so did the venerable Marina when she took refuge in a men's convent. There are many other cases of the same thing. It is called a saving pretence."

While all this was happening and we sat talking the matter over we saw four men driving up the road with a pair of horses and coming straight towards us at a gallop. They seized the girl and put her in the cart, and one of them drove off with her. The other three tied my hands together and haled me back to the village where I had spent the summer. Their only reply to everything I said for myself was to shout, "We'll teach the little saint to seduce young girls!"

[5] *Zavalina.* A bank of earth against the front wall of the house, flat-topped and used as a seat.

That evening they brought me to the village court, put my feet in irons and lodged me in gaol to await my trial in the morning. The priest heard that I was in prison and came to see me. He brought me some supper and comforted me, saying that he would do what he could for me, and give his word as a spiritual father that I was not the sort of person they thought. After sitting with me for a while, he went away.

The magistrate came late in the evening, driving through the village on his way to somewhere else, and stopped at the deputy's house, where they told him what had happened. He bade the peasants come together, and had me brought to the house which was used as a court. We went in and stood waiting. In comes the magistrate, blustering, and sits down on the table with his hat on. "Hi! Epiphan," he shouts, "did the girl, this daughter of yours, run off with anything from your house?"

"No, sir, nothing," was the answer.

"Has she been found out doing anything wrong with that fool there?"

"No, sir."

"Well then, this is my decision and my judgment in the matter; you deal with your daughter yourself, and as for this fellow we will teach him a lesson tomorrow and throw him out of the village, with strict orders never to show his face here again. So that's that."

So saying, he got down from the table and went off to bed, while I was taken back to gaol. Early in the morning two country policemen came, flogged me and drove me out of the village. I went off thanking God that He counted me worthy to suffer for His Name. This comforted me and gave still more warmth and glow to my ceaseless interior prayer. None of these things made me feel at all cast down. It was as though they happened to someone else, and I merely watched them. Even the flogging was within my power to bear. The Prayer brought sweetness into my heart, and made me unaware, so to speak, of everything else.

A mile or two further on I met the girl's mother, coming home from market with what she had bought. Seeing me, she told me that the son-in-law to be had withdrawn his suit. "You see, he is annoyed with Akulka for having run away from him." Then she gave me some bread and patties, and I went on my way.

The weather was fine and dry and I had no wish to spend the night in a village. So when I came upon two fenced-in haystacks as I went through the forest that evening, I lay down beneath them for a night's lodging. I fell asleep and dreamed that I was walking along and reading a chapter of St. Anthony the Great from *The Philokalia*. Suddenly my *starets* overtook me and said, "Don't read that, read this," and pointed to these words in the 35th chapter of St. John Karpathisky, "A teacher submits at times to ignominy and endures pain for the sake of his spiritual children." And again he made me note in the 41st chapter, "Those who give themselves most earnestly to prayer, it is they who become the prey of terrible and violent temptations." Then he said, "Take courage and do not be downcast. Remember the Apostle's words, 'Greater is he that is in you than he that is in the world.' You see that you have now had experience of the truth that no temptation is beyond man's strength to resist, and that with the temptation God makes also a way of escape. Reliance upon this divine help has strengthened holy men of prayer and led them on to greater zeal and ardour. They not only devoted their own lives to ceaseless prayer, but also out of the love of their hearts revealed it and taught it to others as opportunity occurred. St. Gregory of Thessalonika speaks of this as follows, 'Not only should we ourselves in accordance with God's will pray unceasingly in the Name of Jesus Christ, but we are bound to reveal it and teach it to others, to everyone in general, religious and secular, learned and simple, men, women and children, and to inspire them all with zeal for prayer without ceasing.' In the same way the venerable Callistus Telicudes says, 'One ought not to keep thoughts about God (*i.e.*, interior prayer) and what is learned by contemplation, and the means of raising the soul on high, simply in one's own mind, but one should make notes of it, put it into writing for general use and with a loving motive.' And the Scriptures say in this connection, *'Brother is helped by brother like a strong and lofty city'* (Prov. xviii, 19). Only in this case it is above all things necessary to avoid self-praise and to take care that the seed of divine teaching is not sown to the wind."

I woke up feeling great joy in my heart and strength in my soul, and I went on my way.

A long while after this something else happened which also I will tell you about if you like. One day—it was the 24th of March to be exact—I felt a very urgent wish to make my communion the next day—that is, on the Feast of the Annunciation of our Lady. I asked whether the church was far away, and was told it was about twenty miles. So I walked for the rest of that day and all the next night in order to get there in time for Mattins. The weather was as bad as it could be, it snowed and rained, there was a strong wind and it was very cold. On my way I had to cross a small stream, and just as I got to the middle the ice gave way under my feet and I was plunged into the water up to my waist. Drenched like this, I came to Mattins and stood through it, and also through the Liturgy which followed, and at which by God's grace I made my communion. In order to spend the day quietly and without spoiling my spiritual happiness, I begged the verger to allow me to stay in his little room until the next morning. I was more happy than I can tell all that day, and my heart was full of joy. I lay on the plank bed in that unheated room as though I were resting on Abraham's bosom. The Prayer was very active. The love of Jesus Christ and of the Mother of God seemed to surge into my heart in waves of sweetness and steep my soul in consolation and triumph. At nightfall I was seized with violent rheumatic pains in my legs, and that brought to my mind that they were soaking wet. I took no notice of it, and set my heart the more to my Prayer, so that I no longer felt the pain. In the morning when I wanted to get up I found that I could not move my legs. They were quite paralysed, and as feeble as bits of string. The verger dragged me down off the bed by main force. And so there I sat for two days without moving. On the third day the verger set about turning me out of his room, "For," said he, "supposing you die here, what a fuss there will be!" With the greatest of difficulty I somehow or other crawled along on my arms and dragged myself to the steps of the church, and lay there. And there I stayed like that for a couple of days. The people who went by passed me without taking the slightest notice either of me or of my pleadings. In the end a peasant came up to me and sat down and talked. And after a while he asked, "What will you give me if I cure you? I had just exactly the same thing once, so I know a medicine for it."

"I have nothing to give you," I answered.

"But what have you got in your bag?"

"Only dried bread and some books."

"Well, what about working for me just for one summer, if I cure you?"

"I can't do any work; as you see, I have only the use of one arm, the other is almost entirely withered."

"Then what can you do?"

"Nothing, beyond the fact that I can read and write."

"Ah! write! well, teach my little boy to write. He can read a little, and I want him to be able to write too. But it costs such a lot, they want twenty roubles to teach him."

I agreed to this, and with the verger's help he carried me away and put me in an old empty bathhouse in his backyard.

Then he set about curing me. And this was his method. He picked up from the floors, the yards, the cesspools, the best part of a bushel of various sorts of putrid bones, bones of cattle, of birds—all sorts. He washed them, broke them up small with a stone, and put them into a great earthen pot. This he covered with a lid which had a small hole in it, and placed upside down on an empty jar sunk in the ground. He smeared the upper pot with a thick coating of clay, and making a pile of wood round it, he set fire to this and kept it burning for more than twenty-four hours, saying as he fed the fire, "Now we'll get some tar from the bones." Next day, when he took the lower jar out of the ground, there had dripped into it through the hole in the lid of the other jar about a pint of thick, reddish, oily liquid, with a strong smell, like living raw meat. As for the bones left in the jar, from being black and putrid they had become white and clean and transparent like mother of pearl. I rubbed my legs with this liquid five times a day. And lo and behold, twenty-four hours later I found I could move my toes; another day and I could bend my legs and straighten them again. On the fifth day I stood on my feet, and with the help of a stick walked about the yard. In a word, in a week's time my legs had become fully as strong as they were before. I thanked God and mused upon the mysterious power which He has given His creatures. Dry, putrid bones, almost brought to dust, yet keeping such vital force, colour, smell, power of acting on living bodies, and as it were giving life to bodies that are half dead! It is a pledge of the future resurrection of the body. How I would like to point this out to that forester with whom I lived, in view of his doubts about the general resurrection!

Having in this way got better from my illness, I began to teach the boy. Instead of the usual copybook work he wrote out the Prayer of Jesus. I made him copy it showing him how to set out the words nicely. I found teaching the lad restful, for during the daytime he worked for the steward of an estate near by, and could only come to me while the steward slept, that is, from daybreak till the Liturgy.

He was a bright boy, and soon began to write fairly well. His employer saw him writing, and asked him who had taught him.

"A one-armed pilgrim who lives in our old bathhouse," said the boy.

The steward, who was a Pole, was interested, and came to have a look at me. He found me reading *The Philokalia,* and started a talk by asking what I was reading. I showed him the book. "Ah," said he, "that's *The Philokalia.* I've seen the book before at our priest's[6] when I lived at Vilna. They tell me, however, that it contains odd sorts of schemes and tricks for prayer written down by the Greek monks. It's like those fanatics in India and Bokhara who sit down and blow themselves out trying to get a sort of tickling in their hearts, and in their stupidity take this bodily feeling for prayer, and

[6] *Priests.* The word *ksendz,* which means a Polish priest of the Roman Catholic Church. The steward, being a Pole was a Roman Catholic.

look upon it as the gift of God. All that is necessary to fulfil one's duty to God is to pray simply, to stand and say the Our Father as Christ taught us. That puts you right for the whole day; but not to go on over and over again to the same tune. That, if I may say so, is enough to drive you mad. Besides, it's bad for your heart."

"Don't think in that way about this holy book, sir," I answered. "It was not written by simple Greek monks, but by great and very holy men of old time, men whom your Church honours also, such as Anthony the Great, Macarius the Great, Mark the spiritual Athlete, John Chrysostom and others. It was from them that the monks of India and Bokhara took over the 'heart method' of interior prayer, only they quite spoilt and garbled it in doing so, as my *starets* explained to me. In *The Philokalia* all the teaching about the practice of prayer in the heart is taken from the Word of God, from the Holy Bible, in which the same Jesus Christ who bade us say the Our Father taught also ceaseless prayer in the heart. For He said, *'Thou shalt love the Lord thy God with all thy heart and with all thy mind,' 'Watch and pray,' 'Abide in Me and I in you.'* And the holy Fathers, calling to witness the holy King David's words in the Psalms, *'O taste and see how gracious the Lord is,'* explain the passsage thus: that the Christian man ought to use every possible means of seeking, and finding, delight in prayer, and ceaselessly to look for consolation in it, and not be content with simply saying 'Our Father' once a day. Let me read to you how these saints blame those who do not strive to reach the gladness of the prayer of the heart. They write that such do wrong for three reasons, first because they show themselves against the Scriptures inspired by God, and secondly because they do not set before themselves a higher and more perfect state of soul to be reached. They are content with outward virtues only, and cannot hunger and thirst for the truth, and therefore miss the blessedness and joy in the Lord. Thirdly because, by letting their mind dwell upon themselves and their own outward virtues they often slip into temptation and pride, and so fall away."

"It is sublime, what you are reading," said the steward, "but it's hardly for us ordinary lay folk, I think!"

"Well, I will read you something simpler, about how people of goodwill, even if living in the world, may learn how to pray without ceasing."

I found the sermon on George the Youth, by Simeon the New Theologian, and read it to him from *The Philokalia*.

This pleased him, and he said, "Give me that book to read at my leisure, and I will have a good look into it some time."

"I will let you have it for twenty-four hours with pleasure," I answered, "but not for longer, because I read it every day, and I just can't live without it."

"Well then, at least copy out for me what you have just read: I will pay you for your trouble."

"I don't want payment," said I. "I will write that out for you for love's sake and in the hope that God will give you a longing for prayer."

I at once and with pleasure made a copy of the sermon I had read. He read it to his wife, and both of them were pleased with it. And so it came about that at times they would send for me, and I would go, taking *The Philokalia* with me, and read to them while they sat drinking tea and listening. Once they asked me to stay to dinner. The steward's wife, who was a kindly old lady, was sitting with us at table eating some fried fish, when by some mischance she got a bone lodged in her throat. Nothing we could do gave her any relief, and nothing would move the bone. Her throat gave her so much pain that a couple of hours later she had to go and lie down. The doctor (who lived twenty miles away) was sent for, and as by this time it was evening, I went home, feeling very sorry for her.

That night, while I was sleeping lightly, I heard my *starets'* voice. I saw no figure, but I heard him say to me, "The man you are living with cured you, why then do you not help the steward's wife? God has bidden us feel for our neighbour."

"I would help her gladly," I answered, "but how? I know no means whatever."

"Well, this is what you must do: from her very earliest years she has had a dislike of oil. She not only will not taste it, but cannot bear even the smell of it without being sick. So make her drink a spoonful of oil. It will make her vomit, the bone will come away, the oil will soothe the sore the bone has made in her throat, and she will be well again."

"And how am I to give it her, if she dislikes it so? She will refuse to drink it."

"Get the steward to hold her head, and pour it suddenly into her mouth, even if you have to use force."

I woke up, and went straight off and told the steward all this in detail. "What good can your oil do now?" said he. "She is hoarse and delirious, and her neck is all swollen."

"Well, at any rate, let us try; even if it doesn't help, oil is at least harmless as a medicine."

He poured some into a wineglass and somehow or other we got her to swallow it. She was violently sick at once, and soon vomited up the bone, and some blood with it. She began to feel easier, and fell into a deep sleep. In the morning I went to ask after her and found her sitting quietly taking her tea. Both she and her husband were full of wonder at the way she had been cured, and even greater than that was their surprise that her dislike of oil had been told me in a dream, for apart from themselves, not a soul knew of the fact. Just then the doctor also drove up, and the steward told him what had happened to his wife, and I in my turn told him how the peasant had cured my legs. The doctor listened to it all and then said, "Neither the one case nor the other is greatly to be wondered at, it is the same natural force which operated in both cases. Still, I shall make a note of it." And he took out a pencil and wrote in his notebook.

After this the report quickly spread through the whole neighbourhood that I was a prophet and a doctor and wizard. There began a ceaseless stream of visitors from all parts to bring their affairs and their troubles to my notice. They brought me presents and began to treat me with respect and to look after my comfort. I bore this for a week, and then, fearing I should fall into vainglory and harmful distractions, I left the place in secret by night.

Thus once more I set out on my lonely way, feeling as

light as if a great weight had been taken off my shoulders. The Prayer comforted me more and more, so that at times my heart bubbled over with boundless love for Jesus Christ, and from my delight in this streams of consolation seemed to flow through my whole being. The remembrance of Jesus Christ was so stamped upon my mind that as I dwelt upon the Gospel story I seemed to see its events before my very eyes. I was moved even to tears of joy, and sometimes felt such gladness in my heart that I am at a loss even how to tell of it.

It happened at times that for three days together I came upon no human dwelling, and in the uplifting of my spirit I felt as though I were alone on the earth, one wretched sinner before the merciful and man-loving God. This sense of being alone was a comfort to me, and it made me feel my delight in prayer much more than when I was mixing with a crowd of people.

At length I reached Irkutsk. When I had prayed before the relics of St. Innocent, I began to wonder where I should go now. I did not want to stay there for a long while, it was a town in which many people lived. I was walking thoughtfully along the street when I came upon a certain merchant belonging to the place. He stopped me saying, "Are you a pilgrim? Why not come home with me?" We went off together and he took me into his richly furnished house and asked me about myself. I told him all about my travels, and then he said, "You ought to go on a pilgrimage to Jerusalem, there are shrines there the like of which are not to be found anywhere else!"

"I should be only too glad to do so," I answered, "but I haven't the money. I can get along on dry land till I come to the sea, but I have no means of paying for a sea voyage, and it takes a good deal of money."

"How would you like me to find the money for you? I have already sent one of our townsfolk there, an old man, last year," said the merchant.

I fell at his feet, and he went on to say, "Listen, I will give you a letter to my son at Odessa. He lives there and has business connections with Constantinople. He will be pleased to give you a passage on one of the vessels to Constantinople, and to tell his agents there to book a passage to Jerusalem for you on another boat, and pay for it. That is not so very expensive."

I was overcome with joy when I heard this, and thanked my benefactor for his kindness. Even more did I thank God for showing me such fatherly love, and for His care for me, a wretched sinner, who did no good either to himself or to anyone else, and ate the bread of others in idleness. I stayed three days with this kindly merchant. As he had promised, he wrote me a letter to his son, so here I am now on my way to Odessa planning to go on till I reach Jerusalem. But I do not know whether the Lord will allow me to venerate His life-giving tomb.

3

JUST before leaving Irkutsk, I went to see my spiritual
father, with whom I had so often talked, and I said to
him, "Here I am actually off to Jerusalem. I have come
to say good-bye, and to thank you for your love for me
in Christ, unworthy pilgrim as I am."

"May God bless your journey," he replied. "But how
is it that you have never told me about yourself, who
you are nor where you come from? I have heard a great
deal about your travels, and I should be interested to
know something about your birth and your life before
you became a pilgrim."

"Why, very gladly," I answered. "I will tell you all
about that also. It's not a very lengthy matter.

"I was born in a village in the government of Orel.
After the death of our parents, there were just the two
of us left, my brother and I, he was ten years old and I
was two. We were adopted by our grandfather, a worthy
old man and comfortably off. He kept an inn which
stood on the main road, and thanks to his sheer goodness of heart, a lot of travellers put up there. My brother, who was a madcap child, spent most of his time running about in the village, but for my part I liked better
to stay near my grandfather. On Sundays and festivals
we used to go to church together, and at home my
grandfather often used to read the Bible, this very Bible
here, which now belongs to me. When my brother grew
up he took to drink. Once when I was seven years old
and we were both of us lying down on the stove, he
pushed me so hard that I fell off and hurt my left arm,
so that I have never been able to use it since, it is all
withered up. My grandfather saw that I should never be
fit to work on the land and taught me to read. As we

had no spelling-book, he did so from this Bible. He pointed out the A's, and made me form words and learn to know the letters when I saw them. I scarcely know how myself, but, somehow, by saying things after him over and over again, I learned to read in the course of time. And later on, when my grandfather's sight grew weak he often made me read the Bible aloud to him, and he corrected me as he listened. There was a certain clerk who often came to our inn. He wrote a good hand and I liked watching him write. I copied his writing, and he began to teach me. He gave me paper and ink, he made me quill pens, and so I learned to write also. Grandfather was very pleased, and charged me thus, 'God has granted you the gift of learning; it will make a man of you. Give thanks to God, and pray very often.'

"We used to attend all the services at church and we often had prayers at home. It was always my part to read the fifty-first psalm, and while I did so grandfather and grandmother made their prostrations or knelt. When I was seventeen I lost my grandmother. Then grandfather said to me, 'This house of ours no longer has a mistress, and that is not well. Your brother is a worthless fellow. I am going to look for a wife for you, you must get married.' I was against the idea, saying that I was a cripple, but my grandfather would not give way. He found a worthy and sensible young girl about twenty years of age and I married her. A year later my grandfather fell very ill. Knowing that his death was near, he called for me, and bade me farewell, saying, 'I leave you my house and all I have. Obey your conscience, deceive no one, and above all pray to God; everything comes from Him. Trust in Him only. Go to church regularly, read your Bible, and remember me and your grandmother in your prayers. Here is my money, that also I give you; there is a thousand roubles. Take care of it. Do not waste it, but do not be miserly either; give some of it to the poor and to God's church.' After this he died, and I buried him.

"My brother grew envious because the property had been left wholly to me. His anger against me grew, and the Enemy prompted him in this to such an extent that he even laid plains to kill me. In the end this is what he did one night while we were asleep and no guests were in the house. He broke into the room where the money was kept, stole the money from a chest and then set fire to the room. The fire had got a hold upon the whole building before we knew of it, and we only just escaped by jumping out of a window in our night clothes. The Bible was lying under our pillow, so we snatched it up and took it with us. As we watched our house burning we said to one another, 'Thank God, the Bible is saved, that at least is some consolation in our grief.' So everything we had was burnt, and my brother went off without a trace. Later on we heard that when he was in his cups he boasted of the fact that he had taken the money and burnt the house.

"We were left naked and ruined, absolutely beggars. We borrowed some money as best we could, built a little hut, and took up the life of landless peasants. My wife was clever with her hands. She knitted, spun and sewed. People gave her jobs, and day and night she worked and kept me. Owing to the uselessness of my arm I could not even make bark shoes. She would do her knitting and spinning, and I would sit beside her and read the Bible. She would listen, and sometimes began to cry. When I asked, 'What are you crying about? At least we are alive, thank God!' she would answer, 'It touches me so, that beautiful writing in the Bible.'

"Remembering what my grandfather had bidden us, we often fasted, every morning we said the Acathist of Our Lady, and at night we each made a thousand prostrations to avoid falling into temptation. Thus we lived quietly enough for two years. But this is what is so surprising—although we had no understanding of interior prayer offered in the heart and indeed had never heard of it, but prayed with the tongue only, and made our prostrations without thought like buffoons turning somersaults, yet in spite of all this the wish for prayer was there, and the long prayers we said without understanding did not seem tiring, indeed we liked them. Clearly it is true, as a certain teacher once told me, that a secret prayer lies hidden within the human heart. The man himself does not know it, yet working mysteriously within his soul, it urges him to prayer according to each man's knowledge and power.

"After two years of this sort of life that we were leading, my wife was taken suddenly ill with a high fever. She was given her Communion and on the ninth day of her illness she died. I was now left entirely alone in the world. There was no sort of work that I could do; still I had to live, and it went against my conscience to beg. Beside that, I felt such grief at the loss of my wife that I did not know what to do with myself. When I happened to go into our little hut and caught sight of her clothes or perhaps a scarf, I burst into tears and even fell down senseless. So feeling I could no longer bear my grief living at home, I sold the hut for twenty roubles, and such clothes as there were of my own and my wife's I gave away to the poor. Because of my crippled arm I was given a passport which set me free once for all from public duties, and taking my beloved Bible I set straight off, without caring or thinking where I was going.

"But after a while I began to think where I would go, and said to myself, 'first of all I will go to Kiev. I will venerate the shrines of those who were pleasing to God, and ask for their help in my trouble.' As soon as I had made up my mind to this, I began to feel better, and, a good deal comforted. I made my way to Kiev. Since that time, for the last thirteen years that is, I have gone on wandering from place to place, I have made the round of many churches and monasteries, but nowadays I am taking more and more to wandering over the steppes and fields. I do not know whether God will vouchsafe to let me go to Jerusalem. If it be His will, when the time comes my sinful bones may be laid to rest there."

"And how old are you?"

"Thirty-three."

"Well, dear brother, you have reached the age of Our Lord Jesus Christ!"

4

"But it is good for me to hold me fast
by God, to put my trust in the Lord God."

"THE Russian proverb is true, which says that 'man proposes but God disposes,'" said I, as I came back again to my spiritual father. "I thought that by now I should certainly be on my way to Jerusalem. But see how differently things have fallen out. Something quite unlooked for has happened and kept me in the same place here for another three days. And I could not help coming to tell you about it and to ask your advice in making up my mind about the matter.

It happened like this. I had said good-bye to everybody, and with God's help started on my way. I had got as far as the outskirts of the town when I saw a man I knew standing at the door of the very last house. He was at one time a pilgrim like me, but I had not seen him for about three years. We greeted one another and he asked me where I was going.

"God willing," I answered, "I want to go to Jerusalem."

"Thank God! There is a nice fellow-traveller for you," he said.

"God be with you, and with him too," said I, "but surely you know that it is never my way to travel with other people. I always wander about alone."

"Yes, but listen. I feel sure that this one is just your sort; you will suit each other down to the ground. Now, look here, the father of the master of this house, where I have been taken on as a servant, is going under a vow to Jerusalem, and you will easily get used to each other. He belongs to this town, he's a good old man, and what's more he is quite deaf. So much so that however much you shout, he can't hear a word. If you want to ask him anything you have to write it on a bit of paper, and then he answers. So you see he won't bore you on the road; he won't speak to you; even at home here he grows more and more silent. On the other hand you will be a great help to him on the way. His son is giving him a horse and cart, which he will take as far as Odessa and then sell there. The old man wants to go on foot, but the horse is going as well because he has a bit of luggage, and some things he is taking to the Lord's Tomb. And you can put your knapsack in with them too, of course. Now just think, how can we possibly send an old deaf man off with a horse, all by himself on such a long journey? They have searched and searched for somebody to take him, but they all want to be paid such a lot; besides, there's a risk in sending him with someone we don't know, for he has money and belongings with him. Say 'Yes,' brother, it will really be all right; make up your mind now for the glory of God and the love of your neighbour. I will vouch for you to his people, and they will be too pleased for words; they are kindly folk and very fond of me, I've been working for them for two years now."

All this talk had taken place at the door, and he now took me into the house. The head of the household was there, and I saw clearly that they were quite a worthy and decent family. So I agreed to the plan. So now we have arranged to start with God's blessing, after hearing the Liturgy two days after Christmas. What unexpected things we meet with on life's journey! Yet all the while, God and His Holy Providence guide our actions and over-rule our plans, as it is written, *"It is God which worketh in you both to will and to do."*

On hearing all this, my spiritual father said, "I rejoice with all my heart, dear brother, that God has so ordered it that I should see you again, so unexpectedly and so soon. And since you now have time, I want, in all love, to keep you a little longer, and you shall tell me more about the instructive experiences you have met with in the course of your long pilgrimages. I have already listened with great pleasure and interest to what you told me before."

"I am quite ready and happy to do that," I answered, and I began as follows:

A great many things have happened to me, some good and some bad. It would take a long while to tell of them all, and much I have already forgotten. For I have tried especially to remember only such matters as guided and urged my idle soul to prayer. All the rest I rarely remember; or rather have tried to forget the past, as St. Paul bids us when he says, "*Forgetting the things that are behind and stretching forward to the things that are before, I press on toward the goal of the prize of the high calling.*" My late *starets* of blessed memory also used to say that the forces which are against prayer in the heart attack us from two sides, from the left hand and from the right. That is to say, if the Enemy cannot turn us from prayer by means of vain thoughts and sinful ideas, then he brings back into our minds good things we have been taught, and fills us with beautiful ideas, so that one way or another he may lure us away from prayer, which is a thing he cannot bear. It is called "a theft from the right hand side," and in it the soul, putting aside its converse with God, turns to the satisfaction of converse with self or with created things. He taught me, therefore, not to admit during times of prayer even the most lofty of spiritual thoughts. And if I saw that in the course of the day time had been spent more in improving thought and talk than in the actual hidden prayer of the heart, then I was to think of it as a loss of the sense of proportion, or a sign of spiritual greed. This is above all true, he said, in the case of beginners, for whom it is most needful that time given to prayer should be very much more than that taken up by other sides of the devout life.

Still one cannot forget everything. A matter may have printed itself so deeply in one's mind, that although it has not been actually thought of for a long time, yet it is remembered very clearly. A case in point is the few days' stay that God deemed me worthy to enjoy with a certain devout family in the following manner.

During my wanderings in the Tobolsk Government I

happened to pass through a certain country town. My supply of dried bread had run very low, so I went to one of the houses to ask for some more. The householder said, "Thank God, you have come just at the right moment, my wife has only just taken the bread out of the oven, so there is a hot loaf for you. Remember me in your prayers." I thanked him and was putting the bread away in my knapsack, when his wife, who was looking on, said, "What a wretched state your knapsack is in, it is all worn out. I'll give you another instead." And she gave me a good strong one. I thanked them very heartily and went on. On leaving the town I went into a little shop to ask for a bit of salt, and the shopkeeper gave me a small bag quite full. I rejoiced in spirit and thanked God for leading me, unworthy as I was, to such kindly folk. "Now," thought I, "without having to worry about food I shall be filled and content for a whole week. Bless the Lord, O my soul!"

Three miles or so from this town the road I was following passed through a poor village, where I saw a little wooden church nicely decked out and painted on the outside. As I was going by it I felt a wish to honour God's house, and going into the porch I prayed for a while. On the grass at the side of the church there were playing two little children of five or six years of age. I took them to be the parish priest's children, for they were very nicely dressed. I finished my prayers and went on my way, but I had not gone a dozen paces from the church when I heard a shout behind me. "Dear little beggar! Dear little beggar! Stop!" The two little ones I had seen, a boy and a girl, were calling and running after me. I stopped and they ran up to me and took me by the hand. "Come along to mummy, she likes beggars."

"I'm not a beggar," I told them, "I'm just a passer-by."

"Why have you got a bag, then?"

"That is for the bread I eat on the way."

"All the same you must come. Mummy will give you some money for your journey."

"But where is your mummy?" I asked.

"Down there behind the church, behind that little wood."

They took me into a beautiful garden in the middle of which stood a large country house. We went inside, and how clean and smart it all was! The lady of the house came hurrying to us. "Welcome, welcome! God has sent you to us; and how did you come? Sit down, sit down, dear." With her own hands she took off my knapsack and put it on a table, and made me sit in a very comfortably padded chair. "Wouldn't you like something to eat? Or a cup of tea? Isn't there anything you need?"

"I most humbly thank you," I answered, "but I have a whole bagful of food. It is true that I do take tea, but as a peasant I am not very used to it. I value your heart-felt and kindly welcome even more than the treat you offer me. I shall pray that God may bless you for showing such love for strangers in the spirit of the Gospels."

While I was speaking, a strong feeling came over me, urging me to withdraw within myself again. The Prayer was surging up in my heart, and I needed peace and silence to give free play to this quickening flame of prayer, as well as to hide from others the outward signs which went with it, such as tears and sighs and unusual movements of the face and lips. I therefore got up, saying, "Please excuse me, but I must leave now; may the Lord Jesus Christ be with you and with your dear little children."

"Oh, no! God forbid that you should go away. I won't allow it. My husband, who is a magistrate, will be coming back from town this evening, and how delighted he will be to see you! He reverences every pilgrim as a messsenger of God. If you go away he will be really grieved not to have seen you. Beside that, tomorrow is Sunday, and you will pray with us at the Liturgy, and at the dinner-table take your share with us in what God has sent. On holy days we always have up to thirty guests, and all of them our poor brothers in Jesus Christ. Come now, why have you told me nothing about yourself, where you come from and where you are going? Talk to me, I like listening to the spiritual conversation of devout people. Children, children! Take the pilgrim's knapsack into the oratory, he will spend the night there."

I was astonished as I listened to what she said, and I asked myself whether I was talking with a human being or with a ghost of some sort.

So I stayed, and waited for her husband. I gave her a short account of my travels, and said I was on my way to Irkutsk.

"Why, then, you will have to go through Tobolsk," said the lady, "and my own mother is a nun in a convent there, she is a *skhimnitsa*[7] now. We will give you a letter and she will be glad to see you. A great many people go to consult her on spiritual matters. And you will be able to take her a book by St. John of the Ladder which we have just ordered from Moscow at her request. How nicely it all fits in!"

Soon it was dinner-time, and we sat down to table. Four other ladies came in and began the meal with us. When the first course was ended one of them rose, bowed to the Icon,[8] and then to us. Then she went and fetched the second course and sat down again. Then another of the ladies in the same way went and brought the third course. When I saw this, I said to my hostess, "May I venture to ask whether these ladies are relations of yours?"

"Yes, they are indeed sisters to me; this is my cook,

---

[7] *Skhimnik* (fem. *skhimnitsa*). A monk (nun) of the highest grade. The distinction between simple and solemn vows which has arisen in the West, has never found a place in Orthodox Monasticism. In the latter, Religious are of three grades, distinguished by their habit, and the highest grade is pledged to a stricter degree of asceticism and a greater amount of time spent in prayer. The Russian *skhimnik* is the Greek *megaloschemos*.

[8] *Icon*. The icon or sacred picture occupies a prominent position in Orthodox life. In Russia icons are found not only in churches but in public buildings of all sorts, as well as in private houses. In the devout Russian's room the icon will hang or rest on a shelf diagonally across a corner opposite the door, and a reverence will be made to it by a person entering or leaving the room.

and this the coachman's wife, that one has charge of the keys and the other is my maid. They are all married, I have no unmarried girls at all in my whole household."

The more I saw and heard of all this, the more surprised I was, and I thanked God for letting me see these devout people. I felt the prayer stirring strongly in my heart, so wishing to be alone as soon as I could and not hinder the prayer, I said to the lady as soon as we rose from the table, "No doubt you will rest for a while after dinner, and I am so used to walking that I will go for a stroll in the garden."

"No, I don't rest," she replied. "I will come into the garden with you, and you shall talk to me about something instructive. If you go alone, the children will give you no peace, directly they see you, they will not leave you for a minute, they are so fond of beggars, and brothers in Christ, and pilgrims."

There was nothing for me to do but to go with her. In order to avoid doing the talking myself, when we got into the garden I bowed down to the ground before her and said, "Do tell me, please, have you lived this devout life long, and how did you come to take it up?"

"I will tell you the whole story if you like," was the answer. "You see my mother was a great-grand-daughter of St. Joasaph, whose relics rest at Byelgorod. We had a large town house, one wing of which was rented to a man who was a gentleman but not well off. After a while he died; his wife was left pregnant and herself died in giving birth to a child. The infant was left an orphan and in poverty, and out of pity my mother adopted him. A year later I was born. We grew up together and did lessons together with the same tutors and governesses, and were as used to each other as a real brother and sister. Some while later my father died, and my mother gave up living in town and came with us to live on this estate of hers here. When we grew up, she gave me in marriage to her adopted son, settled this estate on us, and herself took the veil in a convent, where she had a cell built for her. She gave us a mother's blessing, and as her last will and testament she urged us to live as good Christians, to say our prayers fervently, and above all try to fulfil the greatest of God's commandments, that is, the love of one's neighbour, to feed and help our poor brothers in Christ in simplicity and humility, to bring up our children in the fear of the Lord, and to treat our serfs as our brothers. And that is how we have been living here by ourselves for the last ten years now, trying as best we could to carry out mother's last wishes. We have a guesthouse for beggars, and at the present moment there are living in it more than ten crippled and sick people. If you care to, we will go and see them tomorrow."

When she had ended her story, I asked her where the book by St. John of the Ladder was, which she wished to send to her mother. "Come indoors," she said, "and I will find it for you."

We had just sat down and begun to read it when her husband came in, and seeing me, gave me a warm welcome. We kissed each other as two brothers in Christ, and then he took me off to his own room, saying, "Come, dear brother, let us go into my study, and you shall bless my cell. I expect she (pointing to his wife) has been boring you. No sooner does she catch sight of a pilgrim of either sex, or of some sick person, than she is so delighted that she will not leave them day or night. She has been like that for years and years." We went into the study. What a lot of books there were, and beautiful icons, and the life-giving Cross with the Figure life-sized, and the Gospels lying near it! I said a prayer, and then, "You are in God's own Paradise here," I said. "Here is the Lord Jesus Christ Himself, and His most holy Mother, and the blessed Saints! And there," I went on, pointing to the books, "are the divine, living and everlasting words of their teaching. I expect you very often enjoy heavenly converse with them."

"Yes, I admit I am a great lover of reading," he answered.

"What sort of books are they you have here?" I asked.

"I have a large number of religious books," was the answer. "Here you see are the Lives of the Saints for the whole year, and the works of St. John Chrysostom, and Basil the Great, and many other theologians and philosophers. I have a lot of volumes of sermons, too, by celebrated modern preachers. My library is worth about five hundred pounds."

"Haven't you anything on prayer?"

"Yes, I am very fond of reading about prayer. Here is the very latest work on the subject, the work of a Petersburg priest." He took down a book on the Lord's Prayer and we began to read it with great enjoyment. A short while after the lady came in, bringing tea, followed by the children, who dragged in a large silver basket full of biscuits and cakes such as I had never tasted before in my life. My host took the book from me and handed it to his wife, saying, "Now we will get her to read; she reads beautifully, and we will keep our strength up with the tea." So she began reading, and we listened. And as I listened I felt the action of the Prayer in my heart. The longer the reading went on the more the Prayer grew and made me glad. Suddenly I saw something flash quickly before my eyes, in the air as it were, like the figure of my departed *starets*. I stared, and so as to hide the fact I said, "Excuse me, I must have dropped asleep for a moment." Then I felt as though the soul of my *starets* made its way into my own, or gave light to it. I felt a sort of light in my mind, and a number of ideas about prayer came to me. I was just crossing myself and setting my will to put these ideas aside when the lady came to the end of the book and her husband asked me whether I had liked it, so that talking began again. "Very much," I answered, "the 'Our Father' is the loftiest and most precious of all the written prayers we Christians have, for the Lord Jesus Christ Himself gave it to us. And the explanation of it which has just been read is very good, too, only it all deals for the most part with the active side of the Christian life, and in my reading the holy Fathers I have come across a more speculative and mystical explanation of the prayer."

"In which of the Fathers did you read this?"

"Well, in Maxim the Confessor, for example, and in Peter the Damascene, in *The Philokalia*."

"Do you remember it? Tell us about it, please."

"Certainly. The first words of the prayer, 'Our Father which art in Heaven' are explained in your book as a call to brotherly love for one's neighbour, since we are

all children of the one Father, and that is very true. But
in the holy Fathers the explanation goes further and is
more deeply spiritual. They say that when we use these
words we should lift up our mind to heaven, to the
Heavenly Father, and remember every moment that we
are in the presence of God.

"The words 'Hallowed be Thy Name' are explained
in your book by the care we ought to have not to utter
the Name of God except with reverence, nor to use it in
a false oath, in a word that the Holy Name of God be
spoken holily and not taken in vain. But the mystical
writers see here a plain call to inward prayer of the
heart; that is, that the most Holy Name of God may be
stamped inwardly upon the heart and be hallowed by
self-acting prayer and hallow all our feelings and all the
powers of the soul. The words "Thy Kingdom come'
they explain thus—may inward peace and quiet and
spiritual joy come to our hearts. In your book again, the
words 'Give us this day our daily bread' are understood
as asking for what we need for our bodily life, not for
more than that, but for what is needed for ourselves and
for the help of our neighbour. On the other hand, Maxim the Confessor understands by 'daily bread' the feeding of the soul with heavenly bread, *i.e.,* the Word of
God, and the union of the soul with God, by dwelling
upon Him in thought and the unceasing inward prayer
of the heart."

"Ah, but the attainment of interior prayer is a very
big business and almost impossible for lay folk," exclaimed my host; "we are lucky if we manage to say our
ordinary prayers without slothfulness."

"Don't look at it in that way," said I. "If it were out
of the question and quite too hard to do, God would not
have bidden us all do it. His strength is made perfect in
weakness. The holy Fathers, who speak from their own
experience, offer us the means, and make the way to
win the prayer of the heart easier. Of course, for hermits
they give special and higher methods, but for those who
live in the world their writings show ways which truly
lead to interior prayer."

"I have never come across anything of that sort in my
reading," he said.

"If you would care to hear it, may I read you a little from *The Philokalia?*" I asked, taking up my copy. I found Peter the Damascene's article, part 3, page 48, and read as follows: " 'One must learn to call upon the Name of God, more even than breathing—at all times, in all places, in every kind of occupation. The Apostle says, *"Pray without ceasing."* That is, he teaches men to have the remembrance of God in all times and places and circumstances. If you are making something you must call to mind the Creator of all things, if you see the light, remember the Giver of it, if you see the heavens and the earth and the sea and all that is in them, wonder and praise the Maker of them. If you put on your clothes recall Whose gift they are and thank Him Who provides for your life. In short, let every action be a cause of your remembering and praising God, and lo! you will be praying without ceasing and therein your soul will always rejoice.' There, you see, this way of ceaseless prayer is simple and easy and within the reach of everybody so long as he has some amount of human feeling."

They were extraordinarily pleased with this. My host took me in his arms and thanked me again and again. Then he looked at my *Philokalia,* saying, "I must certainly buy myself a copy of this. I will get it at once from Petersburg; but for the moment and in memory of this occasion I will copy out the passage you have just read—you read it out to me." And then and there he wrote it out beautifully. Then he exclaimed, "Why, goodness me! Of course I have an icon of the Damascene!" (It was probably of St. John Demascene.) He picked up a frame, put what he had written behind the glass and hung it beneath the icon. "There," said he, "the living word of the Saint underneath his picture will often remind me to put his wholesome advice into practice."

After this we went to supper. As before, the whole household, men and women, sat down to table with us. How reverently silent and calm the meal was! And at the end of it we all, the children as well, spent a long while in prayer. I was asked to read the "Acathist to Jesus the Heart's Delight." Afterwards the servants went away to bed, and we three were left alone in the room.

Then the lady brought me a white shirt and a pair of stockings. I bowed down at her feet, and said, "The stockings, little mother, I will not take. I have never worn them in my life, we are always so used to *onoochi*.[9]" She hurried off and brought back her old kaftan of thin yellow material, and cut it up into two *onoochi*, while her husband, saying, "And look, the poor fellow's footwear is almost worn out," brought me his new *bashmaki*,[10] large ones which he wore over his top boots. Then he told me to go into the next room, which was empty, and change my shirt. I did so, and when I came back to them again they sat me down on a chair to put my new footwear on, he wrapping my feet and legs in the *onoochi* and she putting on the *bashmaki*. At first I would not let them, but they bade me sit down, saying "Sit down and be quiet, Christ washed His disciples' feet." There was nothing to do but obey, and I began to weep, and so did they. After this the lady went to bed with the children, and her husband and I went to a summerhouse in the garden.

For a long while we did not go to sleep, but lay talking. He began in this way, "Now in God's name and on your conscience tell me the real truth. Who are you? You must be of good birth, and are only assuming a disguise of simplicity. You read and write well, you speak correctly, and are able to discuss things, and these things do not go with a peasant upbringing."

"I spoke the real truth with a sincere heart both to you and to your wife when I told you about my birth, and I never had a thought of lying or of deceiving you. Why should I? As for the things I say, they are not my own, but what I have heard from my departed *starets*, who was full of divine wisdom; or what I have gathered from a careful reading of the holy Fathers. But my ignorance has gained more light from interior prayer than from anything else, and that I have not reached by myself, it has been granted me by the mercy of God and the teaching of my *starets*. And that can be done by

[9] *Onoochi*. Long strips of material, generally coarse linen, which the Russian peasant wraps round his feet and legs instead of wearing stockings.

[10] *Bashmaki*. A kind of shoes.

anyone. It costs nothing but the effort to sink down in silence into the depths of one's heart and call more and more upon the radiant Name of Jesus. Everyone who does that feels at once the inward light, everything becomes understandable to him, he even catches sight in this light of some of the mysteries of the Kingdom of God. And what depth and light there is in the mystery of a man coming to know that he has this power to plumb the depths of his own being, to see himself from within, to find delight in self-knowledge, to take pity on himself and shed tears of gladness over his fall and his spoiled will! To show good sense in dealing with things and to talk with people is no hard matter, and lies within anyone's power, for the mind and the heart were there before learning and human wisdom. If the mind is there, you can set it to work either upon science or upon experience, but if the mind is lacking then no teaching, however wise, and no training will be any good. The trouble is that we live far from ourselves and have but little wish to get any nearer to ourselves. Indeed we are running away all the time to avoid coming face to face with our real selves, and we barter the truth for trifles. We think, 'I would very gladly take an interest in spiritual things, and in prayer, but I have no time, the fuss and cares of life give no chance for such a thing.' Yet which is really important and necessary, salvation and the eternal life of the soul, or the fleeting life of the body on which we spend so much labour? It is that that I spoke of, and that leads to either sense or stupidity in people."

"Forgive me, dear brother, I asked not just out of mere curiosity, but from friendliness and Christian sympathy, and even more because about two years ago I came across a case which gave rise to the question I put to you. It was like this: There came to our house a certain beggar with a discharged soldier's passport. He was old and feeble, and so poor that he was almost naked and barefoot. He spoke little, and in such a simple way that you would take him for a peasant of the steppes. We took him into the guesthouse, but some five days later he fell seriously ill, and so we moved him to this very summerhouse, where we kept him quiet, and my wife and I looked after him and nursed him. But after a while it was plain that he was nearing his end. We prepared him for it, and sent for our priest for his Confession, Communion and Annointing. The day before he died, he got up and asked me for a sheet of paper and a pen, and begged me to shut the door and to let no one in while he wrote his will, which he desired me to send after his death to his son at an address in Petersburg. I was astounded when I saw him write, for not only did he write a beautiful and absolutely cultured hand, but the composition also was excellent, thoroughly correct and showing great delicacy of touch. In fact, I'll read you that will of his to-morrow. I have a copy of it. All this set me wondering, and aroused my curiosity enough to ask him about his origin and his life.

"After making me solemnly vow not to reveal it to anyone until after his death, he told me, for the glory of God, the story of his life. 'I was Prince X——,' he began. 'I was very wealthy and led a most luxurious and dissipated life. After the death of my wife, my son and I lived together, he being happily settled in military service; he was a captain in the Guards. One day when I was getting ready to go to a ball at an important person's house, I was very angry with my valet. Unable to control my temper, I struck him a severe blow on the head and ordered him to be sent away to his village. This happened in the evening, and next morning the valet died from the effects of the blow. This did not affect me very seriously. I regretted my rashness, but soon forgot the whole thing. Six weeks later, though, I began seeing the dead valet; in my dreams to begin with; every night he disturbed me and reproached me, incessantly repeating, "Conscienceless man! You are my murderer!" As time went on I began seeing him when I was awake also, wide awake. His appearances grew more and more frequent with the lapse of time, till the agitation he caused me became almost constant. And in the end he did not appear alone, but I saw at the same time other dead men whom I had treated very badly, and women whom I had seduced. They all reproached me ceaselessly and gave me no peace, to such an extent that

I could neither sleep nor eat nor do anything else. My strength grew utterly exhausted, and my skin stuck to my bones. All the efforts of skilled physicians were of no avail at all. I went abroad for a cure, but after trying it for six months, I was not benefited in the slightest degree, and those torturing apparitions grew steadily worse and worse. I was brought home again more dead than alive. I went through the horrors and tortures of Hell in fullest measure. I had proof then that Hell exists, and I knew what it meant!

" 'While I was in this wretched condition I recognised my own wrong-doing. I repented and made my confession. I gave all my serfs their freedom, and took a vow to afflict myself for the rest of my days with as toilsome a life as possible, and to disguise myself as a beggar. I wanted, because of all my sins, to become the humblest servant of people of the very lowest station in life. No sooner had I resolutely come to this decision than those disturbing visions of mine ceased. I felt such comfort and happiness from having made my peace with God that I cannot adequately describe it. But just as I had been through Hell before, so now I experienced Paradise, and learned what that meant also, and how the Kingdom of God is revealed in our hearts. I soon got perfectly well again and carried out my intention, leaving my native land secretly, furnished with a discharged soldier's passport. And now for the last fifteen years I have been wandering about the whole of Siberia. Sometimes I hire myself out to the peasants for such work as I can do. Sometimes I find sustenance by begging in the Name of Christ. Ah, what blessedness and what happiness and what peace of mind I enjoy in the midst of all these privations! It can be felt to the full only by one who by the mercy of the Great Intercessor has been brought out of Hell into Paradise.'

"When he came to the end of his story he handed me the will to forward to his son, and on the following day he died. And I have a copy of that will in a wallet lying on my Bible. If you would like to read it I will get it for you now. . . . Here you are."

I unfolded it and read thus: "In the Name of God the glorious Trinity, the Father, the Son and the Holy Ghost.

"My dearest Son,

"It is fifteen years now since you saw your father. But though you have had no news of him, he has from time to time found means to hear of you, and cherished a father's love for you. That love impels him to send you these few lines from his deathbed. May they be a life-long lesson to you!

"You know how I suffered for my careless and thoughtless life; but you do not know how I have been blessed in my unknown pilgrimage and filled with joy in the fruits of repentance.

"I die at peace in the house of one who has been good to me, and to you also; for kindnesses showered upon the father must touch the feeling heart of a grateful son. Render to him my gratitude in any way you can.

"In bestowing on you my paternal blessing, I adjure you to remember God and to guard your conscience. Be prudent, kindly and considerate; treat your inferiors as benevolently and amiably as you can; do not despise beggars and pilgrims, remembering that only in beggary and pilgrimage did your dying father find rest and peace for his tormented soul. I invoke God's blessing upon you, and calmly close my eyes in the hope of life eternal, through the mercy of the Great Intercessor for men, Our Lord Jesus Christ.

"Your Father X————."

Thus my host and I lay and chatted together; and in my turn I put a question to him. "I suppose you are not without worries and bothers, with this guesthouse of yours? Of course there are quite a lot of our pilgrim brotherhood who take to the life because they have nothing to do, or from sheer laziness, and sometimes they do a little thieving on the road; I have seen it myself."

"There have not been many cases of that sort," was the answer. "We have for the most part always come across genuine pilgrims. And if we do get the other sort, we welcome them all the more kindly and try the harder to get them to stay with us. Through living with our good beggars and brothers in Christ they often become reformed characters and leave the guesthouse humble and kindly folk. Why, there was a case of that sort not so long ago. He was a man belonging to the lower middle class of our town here, and he went so thoroughly to the bad that it came to the point of everybody driving him away from their doors with a stick and refusing to give him even a crust of bread. He was a drunken, quarrelsome bully, and what is more he stole. That was the sort of person he was when one day he came to us, very hungry, and asked for some bread and wine, for the latter of which he was extraordinarily eager. We gave him a friendly reception and said, 'Stay with us and we will give you as much wine as you like, but only on this condition, that when you have been drinking, you go straight away and lie down and go to sleep. If you get in the slightest degree unruly or troublesome, not only shall we turn you out and never take you back again, but I shall report the matter to the police and have you sent off to a penal settlement as a suspected vagabond.' He agreed to this and stopped with us. For a week or more he certainly did drink a great deal, to his heart's content. But because of his promise and because of his attachment to the wine, which he was afraid of being deprived of, he always lay down to sleep afterwards, or took himself off to the kitchen garden and lay down there quietly enough. When he was sober again the brothers of the guesthouse talked persuasively to him and gave him good advice about learning to control himself, if only little by little to begin with. So he gradually began to drink less, and in the end, some three months later, he became quite a temperate person. He has taken a situation somewhere now, and no longer leads a futile life of dependence on other people's charity. The day before yesterday he came her to thank me."

What wisdom! I thought, made perfect by the guidance of love! and aloud I said, "Blessed be God, who has so shown His grace in the household under your care." After this talk we selpt for an hour or an hour and a half till we heard the bells for Mattins. We got ready and went over to the church. On going in we at once saw the lady of the house, who had been there some time already with her children. We were all present at Mattins, and the Divine Liturgy went straight on afterwards. The head of the house with his little boy and I took our places within the altar,[11] while his wife and the little girl stood near the altar window, where they could see the Elevation of the Holy Gifts. How earnestly they prayed as they knelt and shed tears of joy! And I wept to the full myself as I looked at the light on their faces. After the service was over, the gentlefolk, the priest, the servants and the beggars all went off together to the dining-room. There were some forty or so beggars, and cripples and sick folk and children. They all sat down at one and the same table, and how peaceful and silent it all was! I plucked up my courage, and said quietly to my host, "They read the lives of the saints during meals in monasteries. You might do the same. You've got the whole series of books."

"Let us adopt the plan here, Mary," said he, turning to his wife, "it will be most edifying. I will begin, and read at the first dinner-time, then you at the next, then the *batyushka*,[12] and after that the rest of the brothers who know how to read, in turn."

The priest began to talk and eat at the same time. "I like listening, but as for reading—well, with all respect I should like to be let off. You have no idea what a whirl I live in when I get home, worries and jobs of all sorts, first one thing has to be done and then another, what with a host of children and animals into the bargain— my whole day is filled up with things to do. There's no time for reading or study. I've long ago forgotten even what I learned at the seminary." I shuddered as I heard this, but our hostess, who was sitting near me, took my hand and said, "*Batyushka* talks like that because he is so humble, he always makes little of himself, but he is really a man of most kindly and saintly life. He has been

---

[11] *Altar*. In Orthodox churches, *altar* is the name of that part of the building which is known in the West as the Sanctuary. What Westerners call the *altar* is in the East the *throne* or *holy table*. In Orthodox phraseology the *throne* stands in the *altar*.

[12] *Batyushka*. "Little Father," a familiar and affectionate form of address, applied usually to priests.

a widower for the last twenty years, and is bringing up a whole family of grandchildren. For all that he holds services very frequently." At these words there came into my mind the following saying of Nicetas Stethatus in *The Philokalia.* "The nature of things is judged by the inward disposition of the soul," that is, a man gets his ideas about his neighbours from what he himself is. And he goes on to say, "He who has attained to true prayer and love has no sense of the differences between things: he does not distinguish the righteous man from the sinner, but loves them all equally and judges no man, as God causes His sun to shine and His rain to fall on the just and the unjust."

We fell silent again. Opposite me sat one of the beggars from the guesthouse who was quite blind. The master of the house was looking after him. He cut up his fish for him, gave him his spoon and poured out his soup.

I watched carefully and saw that this beggar always had his mouth open and that his tongue was moving all the time, as though it were trembling. Surely, thought I, he must be one of those who pray. And I went on watching. Right at the end of dinner an old woman was taken ill. It was a sharp attack, and she began to groan. Our host and his wife took her into their bedrooom and laid her on their bed, where the lady stayed to look after her. Her husband meanwhile ordered his carriage and went off at a gallop to the town for a doctor The priest went to fetch the Reserved Sacrament, and we all went our ways.

I felt as it were hungry for prayer, an urgent need to pour out my soul in prayer, and I had not been in quiet nor alone for forty-eight hours. I felt as though there were in my heart a sort of flood struggling to burst out and flow through all my limbs. To hold it back caused me severe, even if comforting, pain in the heart, a pain which needed to be calmed and satisfied in the silence of prayer. And now I saw why those who really practise interior self-acting prayer have fled from the company of men and hidden themselves in unknown places. I saw further why the venerable Isikhi called even the most spiritual and helpful talk mere idle chatter if there were too much of it, just as Ephrem the Syrian says, "Good speech is silver, but silence is pure gold."

As I thought all this over, I made my way to the guesthouse, where everyone was resting after dinner. I went up into the attic, where I quietly rested and prayed.

When the beggars were about again I found the blind man and took him off to the kitchen garden, where we sat down alone and began to talk. "Tell me, please," said I, "do you for the sake of your soul say the Prayer of Jesus?"

"I have said it without stopping for a long while."

"But what sort of feeling do you get from it?"

"Only this, that day or night I cannot live without the Prayer."

"How did God show it you? Tell me about it, tell me everything, dear brother."

"Well, it was like this. I belong to this district and used to earn my living by doing tailoring jobs. I travelled about different provinces going from village to village, and made clothes for the peasants. I happened to stay a fairly long time in one village in the house of a peasant for whose family I was making clothing. One day, a holy day it was, I saw three books lying near the icons, and I asked who it was in the household that could read. 'No one,' they answered; 'those books were left us by an uncle; he knew how to read and write.' I picked up one of the books, opened it at random, and read, as I remember to this very hour, the following words: 'Ceaseless prayer is to call upon the Name of God always, whether a man is conversing, or sitting down, or walking, or making something, or eating, whatever he may be doing, in all places and at all times, he ought to call upon God's name.' Reading that started me thinking how simple that would be for me. I began to say the prayer in a whisper while I was sewing, and I liked it. People living in the same house with me noticed it, and began to make fun of me. 'Are you a wizard or what?' they asked, 'going on whispering all the time?' or 'What are you muttering charms about?' So to hide what I was doing I gave up moving my lips and went on saying the Prayer with my tongue only. In the end I got so used to the Prayer that my tongue went on saying it by itself day and night, and I liked it. I went about like that for a long while, and then all of a sudden I became quite blind. Almost everyone in our family gets 'dark water'[13] in the eyes. So, because I was so poor, our people got me into the almshouse at Tobolsk, which is the capital of our province. I am on my way there now, only the gentry have kept me here because they want to give me a cart as far as Tobolsk."

"What was the name of the book you read? Wasn't it called *The Philokalia?*"

"Honestly, I don't know. I didn't even look at the title page."

I fetched my *Philokalia* and looked out in part 4 those very words of the Patriarch Callistus which he had said by heart, and I read them to him.

"Why, those are the very same words!" cried the blind man. "How splendid! Go on reading, brother."

When I got to the lines, "One ought to pray with the heart," he began to ply me with questions. "What does that mean? How is that done?"

I told him that full teaching on praying with the heart was given in this same book, *The Philokalia.* He begged me eagerly to read the whole thing to him.

"This is what we will do," said I. "When are you starting for Tobolsk?"

"Straight away," he answered.

"Very well then, I am also going to take the road again to-morrow. We will go together and I will read it all to you, all about praying with the heart, and I will show you how to find where your heart is, and to enter it."

"And what about the cart?" he asked.

"What does the cart matter! We know how far it is to Tobolsk, a mere hundred miles. We will take it easy, and think how nice it will be going along, just we two together alone, talking and reading about the Prayer as we go." And so it was agreed.

In the evening our host came himself to call us all to supper, and after the meal we told him that the blind

[13] *Dark water.* The popular name for glaucoma.

man and I were taking the road together, and that we did not need a cart, so as to be able to read *The Philokalia* more easily. Hearing this he said, "I also like *The Philokalia* very much, and I have already written a letter and got the money ready to send to Petersburg when I go into court to-morrow, so as to get a copy sent me by return of post."

So we set off on our way next morning, after thanking them very warmly for their great love and kindness. Both of them came with us for more than half a mile from their house. And so we bade each other goodbye.

We went on, the blind man and I, by easy stages, doing from six to ten miles a day. All the rest of the time we spent sitting down in lonely places and reading *The Philokalia*. I read him the whole part about praying with the heart, in the order which my departed *starets* had shown me, *i.e.*, beginning with the writings of Nicephorus the Monk, Gregory of Sinai, and so on. How eagerly and closely he listened to it all, and what happiness and joy it brought him! Then he began to put such questions to me about prayer as my mind was not equal to finding answers to. When we had read what we needed from *The Philokalia* he eagerly begged me actually to show him the way the mind finds the heart, how to bring the Divine Name of Jesus Christ into it, and how to find the joy of praying inwardly with the heart. And I told him all about it thus, "Now you, as a blind man, can see nothing. Yet as a matter of fact you can imagine with your mind and picture to yourself what you have seen in time past, such as a man or some object or other, or one of your own limbs. For instance, can you not picture your hand or your foot as clearly as if you were looking at it, can you not turn your eyes to it and fix them upon it, blind as they are?"

"Yes, I can," he answered.

"Then picture to yourself your heart in just the same way, turn your eyes to it just as though you were looking at it through your breast, and picture it as clearly as you can. And with your ears listen closely to its beating, beat by beat. When you have got into the way of doing this, begin to fit the words of the Prayer to the beats of the heart one after the other, looking at it all the time. Thus, with the first beat, say or think 'Lord,' with the second, 'Jesus,' with the third, 'Christ,' with the fourth, 'have mercy,' and with the fifth 'on me.' And do it over and over again. This will come easily to you, for you already know the groundwork and the first part of praying with the heart. Afterwards, when you have grown used to what I have just told you about, you must begin bringing the whole Prayer of Jesus into and out of your heart in time with your breathing, as the Fathers taught. Thus, as you draw your breath in, say, or imagine yourself saying, 'Lord Jesus Christ,' and as you breathe again, 'have mercy on me.' Do this as often and as much as you can, and in a short space of time you will feel a slight and not unpleasant pain in your heart, followed by a warmth. Thus by God's help you will get the joy of self-acting inward prayer of the heart. But then, whatever you do, be on your guard against imagination and any sort of visions. Don't accept any of them whatever, for the holy Fathers lay down most strongly that inward prayer should be kept free from visions, lest one fall into temptation."

The blind man listened closely to all this, and began eagerly to do with his heart what I had shown him, and he spent a long while at it, especially during the night-time at our halting places. In about five days' time he began to feel the warmth very much, as well as a happiness beyond words in his heart, and a great wish to devote himself unceasingly to this Prayer which stirred up in him a love of Jesus Christ.

From time to time he saw a light, though he could make out no objects in it. And sometimes, when he made the entrance into his heart, it seemed to him as though a flame, as of a lighted candle, blazed up strongly and happily in his heart, and rushing outwards through his throat flooded him with light; and in the light of this flame he could see even far-off things; and this did indeed happen once. We were walking through a forest, and he was silent, wholly given up to the Prayer. Suddenly he said to me, "What a pity! The church is already on fire; there, the belfry has fallen."

"Stop this vain dreaming," I answered, "it is a temptation to you. You must put all such fancies aside at once. How can you possible see what is happening in the town? We are still seven or eight miles away from it."

He obeyed me and went on with his Prayer in silence. Towards evening we came to the town, and there as a matter of fact I saw several burnt houses and a fallen belfry, which had been built with ties of timber, and people crowding around and wondering how it was that the belfry had crushed no one in its fall. As I worked it out, the misfortune had happened at the very same time as the blind man spoke to me about it. And he began to talk to me on the matter. "You told me," said he, "that this vision of mine was vain, but here you see things really are as I saw them. How can I fail to thank and to love the Lord Jesus Christ, Who shows His grace even to sinners and the blind and the foolish! And I thank you also for teaching me the work of the heart."

"Love Jesus Christ," said I, "and thank Him all you will. But beware of taking your visions for direct revelations of grace. For these things may often happen quite naturally in the order of things. The human soul is not bound by place and matter. It can see even in the darkness, and what happens a long way off, as well as things near at hand. Only we do not give force and scope to this spiritual power. We crush it beneath the yoke of our gross bodies or get it mixed up with our haphazard thoughts and ideas. But when we concentrate within ourselves, when we draw away from everything around us and become more subtle and refined in mind, then the soul comes into its own and works to its fullest power. So what happened was natural enough. I have heard my departed *starets* say that there are people (even such as are not given to prayer, but who have this sort of power, or gain it during sickness) who see light even in the darkest of rooms, as though it streamed from every article in it, and see things by it; who see their doubles and enter into the thoughts of other people. But what does come direct from the grace of God in the case of the prayer of the heart, is so full of sweetness and delight that no tongue can tell of it, nor can it be likened to anything material, it is beyond compare. Every feeling is base compared with the sweet knowledge of grace in the heart."

My blind friend listened eagerly to this, and became still more humble. The prayer grew more and more in his heart, and delighted him beyond words. I rejoiced at this with all my soul, and thanked God from my heart that He had let me see so blessed a servant of His. We got to Tobolsk at last. I took him to the almshouse, and leaving him there with a loving farewell, I went on my own way.

I went along without hurrying for about a month with a deep sense of the way in which good lives teach us and spur us on to copy them. I read *The Philokalia* a great deal, and there made sure of everything I had told the blind man of prayer. His example kindled in me zeal and thankfulness and love for God. The Prayer of my heart gave me such consolation that I felt there was no happier person on earth than I, and I doubted if there could be greater and fuller happiness in the kingdom of Heaven. Not only did I feel this in my own soul, but the whole outside world also seemed to me full of charm and delight. Everything drew me to love and thank God; people, trees, plants, animals. I saw them all as my kins-folk, I found in all of them the magic of the Name of Jesus. Sometimes I felt as light as though I had no body and was floating happily through the air instead of walk-ing. Sometimes when I withdrew into myself I saw clear-ly all my internal organs, and was filled with wonder at the wisdom with which the human body is made. Some-times I felt as joyful as if I had been made Tsar. And at all such times of happiness, I wished that God would let death come to me quickly, and let me pour out my heart in thankfulness at His feet in the world of spirits.

It would seem that somehow I took too great a joy in these feelings, or perhaps it was just allowed by God's will, but for some time I felt a sort of quaking and fear in my heart. Was there, I wondered, some new misfor-tune or trouble coming upon me like what happened af-ter I met the girl again to whom I taught the Prayer of Jesus in the chapel? A cloud of such thoughts came down upon me, and I remembered the words of the ven-erable John Karpathisky, who says that "The master will often submit to humiliation and endure disaster and temptation for the sake of those who have profited by him spiritually." I fought against the gloomy thoughts, and prayed with more earnestness than ever. The Prayer quite put them to flight, and taking heart again I said, "God's will be done, I am ready to suffer whatever Jesus Christ sends me for my wickedness and pride. And those to whom I had lately shown the secret of entry into the heart and interior prayer had even before their meeting with me been made ready by the direct and secret teaching of God."

Calmed by these thoughts, I went on my way again filled with consolation, having the Prayer with me and happier even than I had been before. It rained for a couple of days, and the road was so muddy that I could hardly drag my feet out of the mire. I was walking across the steppe, and in ten miles or so I did not find a single dwelling. At last towards nightfall I came upon one house standing by itself right on the road. Glad I was to see it, and I thought I would ask for a rest and a night's lodging here and see what God sent for the morrow; perhaps the weather would get better. As I drew near I saw a tipsy old man in a soldier's cloak sitting on the *zavalina.* I greeted him, saying, "Could I perhaps ask someone to give me a night's lodging here?"

"Who else could give it you but me?" he shouted. "I'm master here. This is a post-house and I am in charge of it."

"Then will you allow me, sir, to spend the night at your house?"

"Have you got a passport? Give some legal account of yourself."

I handed him my passport, and, holding it in his hands, he again asked, "Where is your passport?"

"You have it in your hands," I answered.

"Well, come into the house," said he.

He put his spectacles on, read the passport through, and said, "All right, that's all in order. Stay the night. I'm a good fellow really. Have a drink."

"I don't drink," I answered, "and never have."

"Well, please yourself, I don't care. At any rate have supper with us."

They sat down to table, he and the cook, a young woman who also had been drinking rather freely, and asked me to sit down with them. They quarrelled all through supper, hurling reproaches at each other, and in the end came to blows. The man went off into the passage and to his bed in a lumber-room, while the cook began to tidy up and wash up the cups and spoons, all the while going on with the abuse of her master. I took a seat, thinking it would be some time before she quieted down. So I asked her where I could sleep, for I was very tired from my journey. "I will make you up a bed," she answered. And she placed another bench against the one under the front window, spread a felt blanket over them, and gave me a pillow. I lay down and shut my eyes as though asleep. For a long while yet the cook bustled about, but at last she tidied up, put out the fire, and was coming over towards me. Suddenly the whole window, which was in a corner at the front of the house, frame, glass and splinters of wood, flew into shivers which came showering down with a frightful crash. The whole house shook, and from outside the window came a sickening groan, and shouts and the noise of struggling. The woman sprang back in terror into the middle of the room and fell in a heap on the floor. I jumped up with my wits all astray, thinking the earth had opened under my feet. And the next thing I see is two drivers carrying a man into the house so covered with blood that you could not even see his face. And this added still more to my horror. He was a king's messenger who had galloped here to change horses. His driver had not taken the turn into the gateway properly, the carriage pole stove in the window, and as there was a ditch in front of the house, the carriage overturned and the king's messenger was thrown out, cutting his head badly on a sharp post.

He asked for some water and wine to bathe his wound. Then he drank a glass, and cried, "Horses!"

I went up to him and said, "Surely, sir, you won't travel any further with a wound like that?"

"A king's messenger has no time to be ill," he answered, and galloped off.

The drivers dragged the senseless woman into a corner near the stove, and covered her with a rug, saying, "She was badly scared. She'll come round all right." The master of the house had another glass, and went back to bed, and I was left alone. Very soon the woman got up again and began walking across the room from corner to corner in a witless sort of way, and in the end she went out of the house. I felt as though the shock had taken all the strength out of me, and after saying my prayers I dropped asleep for a while before dawn.

In the morning I took leave of the old man and set off again, and as I walked I sent up my Prayer with faith and trust and thanks to the Father of all blessing and consolation Who had saved me when I was in such great danger.

Some six years after this happened I was passing a convent and went into the church to pray. The kindly abbess welcomed me in her room after the Liturgy, and had tea served. Suddenly some unexpected guests came to see her, and she went to them, leaving me with some of the nuns who waited on her in her cell. One of them, who was pouring out tea, and was clearly a humble soul, made me curious enough to ask whether she had been in the convent long.

"Five years," she answered. "I was out of my mind when they brought me here, and it was here that God had mercy on me. The mother abbess kept me to wait on her in her cell and led me to take the veil."

"How came you to go out of your mind?" I asked.

"It was fright," said she. "I used to work at a post-house and late one night some horses stove in a window. I was so terrified that it drove me out of my mind. For a whole year my relations took me from one shrine to another, but it was only here that I got cured." When I heard this I rejoiced in spirit, and praised God, Who so wisely orders all things for the best.

"I had a great many other experiences," I said, speaking to my spiritual father, "but I should want three whole days and nights to tell you everything as it happened. Still there is one other thing I will tell you about."

One clear summer's day I noticed a cemetery near the road, and what they call a *pogost, i.e.,* a church with some houses for those who minister in it. The bells were ringing for the Liturgy, and I made my way towards it. People who lived round about were going the same way, and some of them, before they got as far as the church, were sitting on the grass. Seeing me hurrying along, they said to me, "Don't hurry, you'll have plenty of time for standing about when the service begins. Services take a long while here: our priest is in bad health and goes very slowly."

The service did, in fact, last a very long while. The priest was a young man, but very thin and pale. He celebrated very slowly indeed, but with great devotion, and at the end of the Liturgy he preached with much feeling a beautiful and simple sermon on how to grow in love for God. The priest asked me into his house and to stay to dinner.

During the meal I said, "How reverently and slowly you celebrate, Father!" "Yes," he answered, "but my parishioners do not like it, and they grumble. Still, there's nothing to be done about it. I like to meditate on each prayer and rejoice in it before I say it aloud. Without that interior appreciation and feeling every word uttered is useless both to myself and to others. Everything centres in the interior life, and in attentive prayer! Yet how few concern themselves with the interior life," he went on.

"It is because they feel no desire to cherish the spiritual inward light."

"And how is one to reach that?" I asked. "It would seem to be very difficult."

"Not at all," was the reply. "To attain spiritual enlightenment and become a man of recollected interior life, you should take some one text or other of Holy Scripture and for as long a period as possible concentrate on that alone all your power of attention and meditation; then the light of understanding will be revealed to you. You must proceed in the same way about prayer. If you want it to be pure, right and enjoyable, you must choose some short prayer, consisting of few but forcible words, and repeat it frequently and for a long while. Then you will find delight in prayer."

This teaching of the priest pleased me very much. How practical and simple it was, and yet at the same time how deep and how wise. I gave thanks to God, in my thoughts, for showing me such a true pastor of his church.

When the meal was over, he said to me, "You have a sleep after dinner while I read the Bible and prepare my sermon for to-morrow." So I went into the kitchen. There was no one there except a very old woman sitting crouched in a corner coughing. I sat down under a small window, took *The Philokalia* out of my knapsack, and began to read quietly to myself. After a while I heard the old woman who was sitting in the corner ceaselessly whispering the Prayer of Jesus. It gave me great joy to hear the Lord's holy Name spoken so often, and I said to her, "What a good thing it is, mother, that you are always saying the Prayer. It is a most Christian and most wholesome action."

"Yes," she replied. "The 'Lord have mercy' is the only thing I have to lean on in my old age."

"Have you made a habit of this prayer for long?"

"Since I was quite young; yes, and I couldn't live without it, for the Jesus Prayer saved me from ruin and death."

"How? Please tell me about it, for the glory of God and in praise of the blessed power of the Prayer of Jesus."

I put *The Philokalia* away in my knapsack and took a seat nearer to her, and she began her story.

"I used to be a young and pretty girl. My parents gave me in marriage, and the very day before the wedding, my bridegroom came to see us. Suddenly, before he had taken a dozen steps, he dropped down and died, without a single gasp. This frightened me so that I utterly refused to marry at all. I made up my mind to live unmarried, to go on pilgrimage to the shrines, and pray at them. However, I was afraid to travel all by myself, young as I was, I feared evil people might molest me. But an old woman-pilgrim whom I knew taught me wherever my road took me always to say the Jesus Prayer without stopping, and told me for certain that if I did no misfortune of any sort could happen to me on my way. I proved the truth of this, for I walked even to far-off shrines and never came to any harm. My parents gave me the money for my journeys. As I grew old I lost my health, and now the priest here out of the kindness of his heart gives me board and lodging."

I was overjoyed to hear this, and knew not how to thank God for this day, in which I had been taught so much by examples of spiritual life. Then, asking the kindly and devout priest for his blessing, I set off again on my way rejoicing.

Then again, not so long ago, as I was making my way here through the Kazan Government, I had a chance of learning how the power of prayer in the Name of Jesus Christ is shown clearly and strongly even in those who use it without a will to do so, and how saying the Prayer often and for a long time is a sure and rapid way to gaining its blessed fruits. It happened that I was to pass the night at a Tartar village. On reaching it I saw a Russian carriage and coachman outside the window of one of the huts. The horses were being fed near by. I was glad to see all this, and made up my mind to ask for a night's lodging at the same place, thinking that I should at least spend the night with Christians.[14] When I came up to them I asked the coachman where he was going, and he answered that his master was going from Kazan to the Crimea. While I was talking with the coachman his master pulled open the carriage curtains from inside, looked out and saw me. Then he said, "I shall stay the night here, too, but I have not gone into the hut, Tartar houses are so uncomfortable. I have decided to spend the night in the carriage." Then he got out, and as it was a fine evening, we strolled about for a while and talked. He asked me a lot of questions and talked about himself also, and this is what he told me. "Until I was sixty-five I was a captain in the navy, but as I grew old I became the victim of gout—an incurable disease. So I retired from the service and lived, almost constantly ill, on a farm of my wife's in the Crimea. She was an impulsive woman of a volatile disposition, and a great card-player. She found it boring living with a sick man, and left me, going off to our daughter in Kazan, who happened to be married to a civil servant there. My wife laid hands on

[14] The Tartars, of course, being Moslems.

all she could, and even took the servants with her, leaving me with nobody but an eight-year-old boy, my godson. So I lived alone for about three years. The boy who served me was a sharp little fellow, and capable of doing all the household work. He did my room, heated the stove, cooked the gruel and got the samovar[15] ready. But at the same time he was extraordinarily mischievous and full of spirits. He was incessantly rushing about and banging and shouting and playing, and up to all sorts of tricks, so that he disturbed me exceedingly. And I, being ill and bored, liked to read spiritual books all the time. I had one splendid book by Gregory Palamas, on the Prayer of Jesus. I read it almost continously, and I used to say the Prayer to some extent. But the boy hindered me, and no threats and no punishment restrained him from indulging in his pranks. At last I hit upon the following method. I made him sit on a bench in my my room with me, and bade him say the Prayer of Jesus without stopping. At first this was extraordinarily distasteful to him, and he tried all sorts of ways to avoid it, and often fell silent. In order to make him do my bidding, I kept a cane beside me. When he said the Prayer I quietly read my book, or listened to how he was saying it. But let him stop for a moment, and I showed him the cane, then he got frightened and took to the Prayer again. I found this very peaceful, and quiet reigned in the house. After a while I noticed that now there was no need of the cane; the boy began to do my bidding quite willingly and eagerly. Further, I observed a complete change in his mischievous character: he became quiet and taciturn and performed his household tasks better than before. I was glad of this, and began to allow him more freedom. And what was the result? Well, in the end he got so accustomed to the Prayer that he was saying it almost the whole time, whatever he was doing, and without any compulsion from me at all. When I asked him about it, he answered that he felt an insuperable desire to be saying the Prayer always.

" 'And what are your feelings while doing so?' I asked him.

[15] *Samovar.* A sort of urn heated with charcoal to supply hot water for tea.

" 'Nothing,' said he, 'only I feel that it's nice to be saying it.'

" 'How do you mean—nice?'

" 'I don't know how to put it exactly.'

" 'Makes you feel cheerful, do you mean?'

" 'Yes, cheerful.'

"He was twelve years old when the Crimean War broke out, and I went to stay with my daughter at Kazan, taking him with me Here he lived in the kitchen with the other servants, and this bored him very much. He would come to me with complaints that the others, playing and joking among themselves, bothered him also, and laughed at him and so prevented him saying his Prayer. In the end, after about three months, he came to me and said, 'I am going home, I'm unbearably sick of this place and all this noise.'

" 'How can you go alone for such a distance and in winter, too?' said I. 'Wait, and when I go I'll take you with me.' Next day my boy had vanished.

"We sent everywhere to look for him, but nowhere could he be found. In the end I got a letter from the Crimea, from the people who were on our farm, saying that the boy had been found dead in my empty house on the 4th of April, which was Easter Monday. He was lying peacefully on the floor of my room with his hands folded on his breast, and in that same thin frockcoat that he always went about my house in, and which he was wearing when he went away. And so they buried him in my garden.

"When I heard this news I was absolutely amazed. How had the child reached the farm so quickly? He started on Feb. 26th, and he was found on April 4th. Even with God's help you want horses to cover 2,000 miles in a month! Why, it is nearly seventy miles a day! And in thin clothes, without a passport and without a farthing in his pocket into the bargain! Even supposing that someone may have given him a lift on the way, still that in itself would be a mark of God's special providence and care for him. That boy of mine, mark you, enjoyed the fruits of prayer," concluded the gentleman, "and here am I, an old man, still not as far on as he."

Later on I said to him, "It is a splendid book, sir, the

one by Gregory Palamas, which you said you liked reading. I know it. But it treats rather of the oral Prayer of Jesus. You should read a book called *The Philokalia.* There you will find a full and complete study of how to reach the spiritual Prayer of Jesus in the mind and heart also, and taste the sweet fruit of it." At the same time I showed him my *Philokalia.* I saw that he was pleased to have this advice of mine, and he promised that he would get a copy for himself. And in my own mind I dwelt upon the wonderful ways in which the power of God is shown in this Prayer. What wisdom and teaching there was in the story I had just heard! The cane taught the Prayer to the boy, and what is more, as a means of consolation it became a help to him. Are not our own sorrows and trials which we meet with on the road of prayer in the same way the rod in God's hand? Why then are we so frightened and troubled when our heavenly Father in the fullness of His boundless love lets us see them, and when these rods teach us to be more earnest in learning to pray, and lead us on to consolation which is beyond words?

When I came to the end of the things I had to tell, I said to my spiritual father: "Forgive me, in God's name. I have already chattered far too much. And the holy Fathers call even spiritual talk mere babble if it lasts too long. It is time I went to find my fellow-traveller to Jerusalem. Pray for me, a miserable sinner, that of His great mercy God may bless my journey."

"With all my heart I wish it, dear brother in the Lord," he replied. "May all the all-loving Grace of God shed its light on your path, and go with you, as the Angel Raphael went with Tobias!"

THE PILGRIM CONTINUES
HIS WAY

5

THE STARETS. *A year had gone by since I last saw the Pilgrim, when at length a gentle knock on the door and a pleading voice announced the arrival of that devout brother to the hearty welcome which awaited him.*

"Come in, dear brother; let us thank God together for blessing your journey and bringing you back."

The Pilgrim. Praise and thanks be to the Father on high for His bounty in all things, which He orders as seems good to Him, and always for the good of us pilgrims and strangers in a strange land. Here am I, a sinner, who left you last year, again by the mercy of God thought worthy to see and hear your joyful welcome. And of course you are waiting to hear from me a full account of the Holy City of God, Jerusalem, for which my soul was longing and towards which my purpose was firmly set. But what we wish is not always carried out; and so it was in my case. And no wonder, for why should I, a wretched sinner, be thought fit to tread that holy ground on which the divine footsteps of our Lord Jesus Christ were printed?

You remember, Father, that I left here last year with a deaf old man as a companion, and that I had a letter from a merchant of Irkutsk to his son at Odessa asking him to send me to Jerusalem. Well, we got to Odessa all right in no very long time. My companion at once booked a passage on a ship for Constantinople and set off. I for my part set about finding the merchant's son, by the address on the letter. I soon found his house, but there, to my surprise and sorrow, I learned that my benefactor was no longer alive. He had been dead and buried three weeks before, after a short illness. This made me very much cast down. But still, I trusted in the power of God. The whole household was in mourning, and the widow, who was left with three small children, was in such distress, that she wept all the time, and several times a day would collapse in grief. Her sorrow was so great that it seemed as though she too would not live long. All the same, in the midst of all this, she met me kindly, though in such a state of affairs she could not send me to Jerusalem. But she asked me to stay with her for a fortnight or so until her father-in-law came to Odessa, as he had promised, to settle the affairs of the bereaved family.

So I stayed. A week passed, a month, then another. But instead of coming the merchant wrote to say that his own affairs would not allow him to come, and advising that she should pay off the assistants, and that all should go to him at Irkutsk at once. So a great bustle and fuss began, and as I saw they were no longer interested in me, I thanked them for their hospitality and said goodbye. Once more I set off wandering about Russia.

I thought and thought. Where was I to go now? In the end I decided that first of all I would go to Kiev, where I had not been for many years. So I set off. Of course I fretted at first because I had not been able to carry out my wish to go to Jerusalem, but I reflected that even this had not happened without the providence of God, and I quieted myself with the hope that God, the lover of men, would take the will for the deed, and would not let my wretched journey be without edification and spiritual value. And so it turned out, for I came across the sort of people who showed me many things that I did not know, and for my salvation brought light to my dark soul. If that necessity had not sent me on this journey I should not have met those spiritual benefactors of mine.

So by day I walked along with the Prayer, and in the evening when I halted for the night I read my *Philokalia,* for the strengthening and stimulating of my soul in its struggle with the unseen enemies of salvation.

On the road about forty-five miles from Odessa I met with an astonishing thing. There was a long train of wagons loaded with goods; there were about thirty of them, and I overtook them. The foremost driver, being the leader, was walking beside his horse, and the others were walking in a group some way from him. The road led past a pond which had a stream running through it, and in which the broken ice of the spring season was whirling about and piling up on the edges with a horrible noise. All of a sudden, the leading driver, a young man, stopped his horse, and the whole line of carts behind had to come to a standstill too. The other drivers came running up to him, and saw that he had begun to undress. They asked him why he was undressing. He answered that he very much wanted to bathe in the pond. Some of the astonished drivers began to laugh at him, others to scold him, calling him mad, and the eldest there, his own brother, tried to stop him, giving him a push to make him drive on. The other defended himself and had not the least wish to do as he was told. Several of the young drivers started getting water out of the pond in the buckets with which they watered the horses, and for a joke splashed it over the man who wanted to bathe, on his head, or from behind, saying, "There you are; we'll give you a bath." As soon as the water touched his body, he cried out, "Ah, that's good," and sat down on the ground. They went on throwing water over him. Thereupon he soon lay down, and then and there quietly died. They were all in a great fright, having no idea why it had happened. The older ones bustled about, saying that the authorities ought to be told, while the rest came to the conclusion that it was his fate to meet this kind of death.

I stayed with them about an hour and then went on my way. About three and a half miles farther on I saw a village on the high road, and as I came into it I met an old priest walking along the street. I thought I would tell him about what I had just seen, and find out what he thought about it. The priest took me into his house, and I told him the story and asked him to explain to me the cause of what had taken place.

"I can tell you nothing about it, dear brother, except perhaps this, that there are many wonderful things in nature which our minds cannot understand. This, I think, is so ordered by God in order to show men the rule and providence of God in nature more clearly, through certain cases of unnatural and direct changes in its laws. It happens that I myself was once a witness of a similar case. Near our village there is a very deep and steep-sided ravine, not very wide, but some seventy feet or more in depth. It is quite frightening to look down to the gloomy bottom of it. A sort of footbridge has been built over it. A peasant in my parish, a family man and very respectable, suddenly, for no reason, was taken with an irresistible desire to throw himself from this little bridge into that deep ravine. He fought against the idea and resisted the impulse for a whole week. In the end, he could hold himself back no longer. He got up early, rushed off and jumped into the abyss. They soon heard his groans, and with great difficulty pulled him out of the pit with his legs broken. When he was asked the reason for his fall, he answered that although he was now feeling a great deal of pain, yet he was calm in spirit, that he had carried out the irresistible desire which had worried him so for a whole week, and that he had been ready to risk his life to gratify his wish.

"He was a whole year in hospital getting better. I used to go to see him, and often saw the doctors who were round him. Like you, I wanted to hear from them the cause of the affair. With one voice the doctors answered that it was 'frenzy.' When I asked them for a scientific explanation of what that was, and what caused it to attack a man, I could get nothing more out of them, except that this was one of the secrets of nature which were not revealed to science. I for my part observed that if in such a mystery of nature a man were to turn to God in prayer, and also to tell good people about it, then this ungovernable 'frenzy' of theirs would not attain its purpose.

"Truly there is much to be met with in human life of which we can have no clear understanding."

While we were talking it was getting dark, and I stayed the night there. In the morning the mayor sent his secretary to ask the priest to bury the dead man in the cemetery, and to say that the doctors, after a *post-mortem,* had found no signs whatever of madness, and gave a sudden stroke as the cause of death.

"Look at that now," said the priest to me, "medical

science can give no precise reason for his uncontrollable urge towards the water."

And so I said good-bye to the priest and went on my way. After I had travelled for several days and was feeling rather done-in, I came to a good-sized commercial town called Byelaya Tserkov. As evening was already coming on, I started to look around for a lodging for the night. In the market I came across a man who looked as though he was a traveller too. He was making enquiries among the shops for the address of a certain person who lived in the place. When he saw me he came up to me and said: "You look as though you are a pilgrim too, so let's go together and find a man by the name of Evreinov who lives in this town. He is a good Christian and keeps a splendid inn, and he welcomes pilgrims. Look, I've got something written down about him." I gladly agreed, and so we soon found his house. Although the host himself was not at home, his wife, a nice old woman, received us very kindly and gave us an out-of-the-way private little garret in the attic to rest in. We settled down and rested for a while.

Then our host came, and asked us to have supper with them. During supper we talked—who we were and where we came from—and somehow or other the talk came round to the question of why he was called Evreinov. "I'll tell you an odd thing about that," he said, and began his story.

"You see, it was like this. My father was a Jew. He was born at Shklov, and he hated Christians. From his very earliest years he was preparing to be a rabbi and studied hard at all the Jewish chit-chat which was meant to disprove Christianity. One day he happened to be going through a Christian cemetery. He saw a human skull, which must have been taken out of some grave that had been recently disturbed. It had both its jaws and there were some horrible-looking teeth in them. In a fit of temper he began to jeer at this skull; he spat at it, abused it and spurned it with his foot. Not content with that, he picked it up and stuck it on a post—as they stick up the bones of animals to drive off greedy birds. After amusing himself in this way, he went home. The following night he had scarcely fallen asleep when suddenly an unknown man appeared to him and violently upbraided him, saying, 'How dare you insult what is left of my poor bones? I am a Christian—but as for you, you are the enemy of Christ.' The vision was repeated several times every night, and he got neither sleep nor rest. Then the same sight started flashing before his eyes during the daytime also, and he would hear the echo of that reproachful voice. As time went on the vision got more frequent, and in the end he began to feel depressed and frightened and to lose strength. He went to his rabbi, who read prayers and exorcisms over him. But the apparition not only did not cease; it got even more frequent and threatening.

"This state of affairs became known, and, hearing about it, a business friend of his, a Christian, began to advise him to accept the Christian religion, and to urge upon him that apart from that there was no way of ridding himself of this disturbing apparition of his. But the Jew was loth to take this step. However, in reply he said: 'I would gladly do as you wish, if only I could be free from this tormenting and intolerable apparition.' The Christian was glad to hear this, and persuaded him to send in to the local Bishop a request for baptism and reception into the Christian Church. The request was written and the Jew, not very eagerly, signed it. And low and behold, the very minute that the request was signed, the apparition came to an end and never troubled him again. His joy was unbounded, and entirely at rest in mind he felt such a burning faith in Jesus Christ that he went straight away to the Bishop, told him the whole story, and expressed a heartfelt desire to be christened. He eagerly and quickly learned the dogmas of the Christian faith, and after his baptism he came to live in this town. Here he married my mother, a good Christian woman. He led a devout and very comfortable life and he was most generous to the poor. He taught me to be the same, and before his death gave me his instructions about this, together with his blessing. There you are; that's why my name is Evreinov."[16]

I listened to this story with reverence and humility,

---

[16] *Evreinov*. Literally the name means "Son of a Jew."

and I thought to myself: "How good and kind our Lord Jesus Christ is, and how great is His love! In what different ways He draws sinners to Himself. With what wisdom He uses things of little importance to lead on to great things. Who could have expected that the mischievous pranks of a Jew with some dead bones would bring him to the true knowledge of Jesus Christ and be the means of leading him to a devout life?"

After supper we thanked God and our host, and retired to our garret. We did not want to go to bed yet, so we went on talking to each other. My companion told me that he was a merchant of Mogilev, and that he had spent two years in Bessarabia as a novice in one of the monasteries there, but only with a passport that expired at a fixed date. He was now on his way home to get the consent of the merchant community to his finally entering upon the monastic life. "The monasteries there satisfy me, their constitution and order, and the strict life of many devout *startsi* who live there." He assured me that putting the Bessarabian monasteries beside the Russian was like comparing heaven with earth. He urged me to do the same.

While we were talking about these things they brought still a third lodger into our room. This was a non-commissioned officer with the army for the time being, but now going home on leave. We saw that he was tired out with his journey. We said our prayers together and lay down to sleep. We were up early next morning and began to get ready for the road, and we only just wanted to go and thank our host, when suddenly we heard the bells ringing for Mattins. The merchant and I began to consider what we would do. How could we start after hearing the bells and without going to church? It would be better to stay to Mattins, say our prayers in church, and then we should go off more happily. So we decided; and we called the officer. But he said: "What's the point of going to church while you are on a journey? What good is it to God if we have been? Let's get off home and then say our prayers. You two go if you want. I'm not going. By the time you have stood through Mattins I shall be three or four miles or so farther on my way, and I want to get home as quickly as possible." To this the merchant said: "Look here, brother, don't you run so far ahead with your schemes until you know what God's plans are!" So we went to church, and he took the road.

We stayed through Mattins and the Liturgy too. Then we went back to our garret to get our knapsacks ready for the start, when what do we see but our hostess bringing in the *samovar*. "Where are you off to?" she says. "You must have a cup of tea—yes, and have dinner with us too. We can't send you away hungry." So we stayed. We had not been sitting at the *samovar* for half an hour, when all of a sudden our non-commissioned officer comes running in, all out of breath.

"I've come to you in both sorrow and joy."

"What's all this?" we asked him.

This is what he said:

"When I left you and started off, I thought I would look in at the pub to get change for a note, and have a drink at the same time so as to get along better. So I did. I got my change, had my drink, and was off like a bird. When I had gone about two miles I had a mind to count the money the fellow at the pub had given me. I sat down by the roadside, took out my pocket-book, and went through it. All serene. Then suddenly it struck me that my passport was not there. Only some papers and the money. I was as frightened as if I'd lost my head. I saw in a flash what had happened. Of course I had dropped it when I was settling up at the pub. I must run back. I ran and ran. Another awful idea seized me: suppose it's not there! that will mean trouble! I rushed up to the man behind the bar and asked him. 'I've not seen it,' he said. And was I downhearted! Well, I searched around and hunted everywhere, wherever I had stood and hung about. And what do you think? I was lucky enough to find my passport. There it was, still folded up and lying on the floor among the straw and litter, all trampled in the dirt. Thank God! I was glad, I can tell you; it was as though a mountain had rolled off my shoulders. Of course it was filthy and coated with mud, enough to get me a clout on the head; still, that doesn't matter. At any rate I can get home and back again with a whole skin. But I came to tell you about it. And what's more, in my fright I've rubbed my foot absolutely raw with running and I can't possibly walk. So I came to ask for some grease to bandage it up with."

"There you are, brother," the merchant began; "that's because you wouldn't listen and come with us to church. You wanted to get a long way ahead of us, and, on the contrary, here you are back again, and lame into the bargain. I told you not to run so far ahead with your schemes; and now see how it has turned out. It was a small thing that you did not come to church, but beside that you used such language as, 'What good does it do God if we pray?' That, brother, was bad, Of course, God does not need our sinful prayers, but, still, in His love for us He likes us to pray. And it is not only that holy prayer which the Holy Spirit Himself helps us to offer and arouses in us that is pleasing to Him, for He asks that of us when He says *Abide in Me, and I in you;* but every intention, every impulse, even every thought which is directed to His glory and our own salvation, is of value in His sight. For all these the boundless loving kindness of God gives bountiful rewards. The love of God gives grace a thousandfold more than human actions deserve. If you give Him the merest mite, He will pay you back with gold. If you but purpose to go to the Father, He will come out to meet you. You say but a word, short and unfeeling—'Receive me, have mercy on me'—and He falls on your neck and kisses you. That is what the love of the Heavenly Father is like towards us, unworthy as we are. And simply because of this love He rejoices in every gesture we make towards salvation, however small. It looks like this to you: What glory is there for God, what advantage for you, if you pray a little and then your thoughts wander again, or if you do some small good deed, such as reading a prayer, making five or ten acts of reverence, or giving a heartfelt sigh and calling upon the Name of Jesus, or attending to some good thought, or setting yourself to some spiritual reading, or abstaining from some food, or bearing an affront in silence—all that seems to you not enough for your full salvation and a fruitless thing to do. No! none of these small acts is in vain; it will be taken into account by the all-seeing eye of God, and receive a hun-

dredfold reward, not only in eternity, but in this life. St.
John Chrysostom asserts this. 'No good of any sort,' he
says, 'however trifling it may be, will be scorned by the
righteous Judge. If sins are searched out in such detail
that we shall give an answer for words and desires and
thoughts, then so much the more good deeds, however
small they are, will be taken into account in all detail,
and will be reckoned to our merit before our Judge, who
is full of love.'

"I will tell you a case which I saw myself last year. In
the Bessarabian monastery where I lived there was a
starets, a monk of good life. One day a temptation beset
him. He felt a great longing for some dried fish. And as
it was impossible to get any in the monastery at that
time, he was planning to go to the market and buy
some. For a long while he struggled against the idea,
and reasoned with himself that a monk ought to be content with the ordinary food provided for the brothers
and by all means to avoid self-indulgence. Moreover, to
walk about the market among crowds of people was also
for a monk a source of temptation, and unseemly. In the
end the lies of the Enemy got the upper hand of his reasoning, and he, yielding to his self-will, made up his
mind and went for the fish. After he had left the building and was going along the street, he noticed that his
rosary was not in his hand, and he began to think: 'How
comes this, that I am going like a soldier without his
sword? This is most unseemly. And lay-folk who meet
me will criticize me and fall into temptation, seeing a
monk without his rosary!' He was going back to get it,
but, feeling in his pocket, he found it there. He pulled it
out, crossed himself, and with his roasary in his hand
went calmly on. As he got near the market he saw a
horse standing by a shop with a great cart-load of enor-
mous tubs. All at once this horse, taking fright at something or other, bolted with all its might and with thun-
dering hoofs made straight for him, grazing his shoulder
and throwing him to the ground, though not hurting him
very much. Then, a couple of paces from him, that load
toppled over and the cart was smashed to splinters. Getting up quickly, naturally he was frightened enough, but
at the same time he marvelled how God had saved his

life, for if the load had fallen a split second earlier, then he would have been smashed to pieces like the cart. Thinking no further about it, he bought the fish, went back, ate it, said his prayers, and lay down to sleep.

"He slept lightly, and in his sleep a benign-looking *starets* whom he did not know appeared to him, and said: 'Listen, I am the protector of this dwelling, and I wish to teach you so that you will understand and remember the lesson now given you. Look now: the feeble effort you made against the feeling of pleasure, and your sloth in self-understanding and self-control, gave the Enemy his chance to attack you. He had got ready for you that fatal bombshell which exploded before your eyes. But your guardian angel foresaw this and put into your mind the thought of offering a prayer and remembering your rosary. Since you listened to this suggestion, obeyed and put it into action, it was just this that saved you from death. Do you see God's love for men, and His bountiful reward of even a slight turning towards Him?' Saying this, the visionary *starets* quickly left the cell. The monk bowed down at his feet, and in doing so woke up, to find himself, not on his bed, but kneeling prostrate at the threshold of the door. He told the story of this vision for the spiritual benefit of many people, myself among them.

"Truly boundless is the love of God for us sinners. Is it not marvellous that so small an action—yes, just taking his rosary out of his pocket and carrying it in his hand and calling once upon the Name of God—that that should give a man his life, and that in the scales of judgment upon men one short moment of calling upon Jesus Christ should outweigh many hours of sloth? In truth, here is the repayment of the tiny mite with gold. Do you see, brother, how powerful prayer is and how mighty the Name of Jesus when we call upon it? St. John Karpathisky in *The Philokalia* says that when in the Prayer of Jesus we call upon the Holy Name and say, 'Have mercy on me, a sinner,' then to every such petition the Voice of God answers in secret, 'Son, thy sins be forgiven thee.' And he goes on to say that when we say the Prayer there is at that moment nothing to distinguish us from the saints, confessors and martyrs. For, as St.

Chrysostom says, 'Prayer, although we are full of sin when we utter it, immediately cleanses us. God's loving-kindness to us is great, yet we sinners are listless, are not willing to give even one small hour to God in thanksgiving, and barter the time of prayer, which is more important than anything, for the bustle and cares of living, forgetting God and our duty. For that reason we often meet with misfortunes and calamities, yet even these the all-loving providence of God uses for our instruction and to turn our hearts to Him.'"

When the merchant came to the end of his talk to the officer, I said to him: "What comfort you have brought to my sinful soul too, your honour! I could bow down to your very feet." Hearing this, he began to speak to me. "Ah, it seems you are a lover of religious stories. Wait a moment and I'll read you another like the one I have just told him. I've got here a book I travel with called *Agapia; or, The Salvation of Sinners*. There are a lot of wonderful things in it."

He took the book out of his pocket and started reading a most beautiful story about one Agathonik, a devout man who from his childhood had been taught by pious parents to say every single day before the icon of the Mother of God the prayer which begins "Rejoice, God-bearing Maiden." And this he always did. Later, when he had grown up and started life on his own, he got absorbed in the cares and fuss of life and said the prayer but rarely, and finally gave it up altogether.

One day he gave a pilgrim a lodging for the night, who told him he was a hermit from the Thebaid and that he had seen a vision in which he was told to go to Agathonik and rebuke him for having given up the prayer to the Mother of God. Agathonik said the reason was that he had said the prayer for many years without seeing any result whatever. Then the hermit said to him: "Remember, blind and thankless one, how many times this prayer has helped you and saved you from disaster. Remember how in your youth you were wonderfully saved from drowning. Do you not recall that an epidemic of infectious disease carried off many of your friends to the grave, but you remained in health? Do you remember, when you were driving with a friend, you both fell out of the cart; he broke his leg, but you were un-hurt? Do you not know that a young man of your ac-quaintance who used to be well and strong is now lying weak and ill, whereas you are in good health and feel no pain?" And he reminded Agathonik of many other things. In the end he said: "Know this, that all those troubles were warded off from you by the protection of the most holy Mother of God because of that short prayer, by which you lifted up your heart every day into union with God. Take care now, go on with it, and do not give up praising the Queen of Heaven lest she should forsake you."

When he had finished reading they called us to din-ner, and afterwards, feeling our strength renewed, we thanked our host and took the road. We parted, and each went his own way as seemed best to him.

After that I walked on for about five days, cheered by the memory of the stories I had heard from the good merchant in Byelaya Tserkov, and I began to get near to Kiev. All at once and for no reason at all I began to feel dull and heavy and my thoughts got gloomy and dispirit-ed. The Prayer went with difficulty and a sort of indol-ence came over me. So, seeing a wood with a thick un-dergrowth of bushes by the side of the road, I went into it to rest a bit, looking for some out-of-the-way place where I could sit under a bush and read my *Philokalia*, and so arouse my feeble spirit and comfort my faint-heartedness. I found a quiet place and began to read Kassian the Roman in the fourth part of *The Philokalia* —on the Eight Thoughts. When I had been reading happily for about half an hour, quite unexpectedly I no-ticed the figure of a man some hundred yards or so away from me and farther in the forest. He was kneeling quite motionless. I was glad to see this, for I gathered, of course, that he was praying, and I began to read again. I went on reading for an hour or more and then glanced up again. The man was still kneeling there and never stirred. All this moved me very much and I thought, What devout servants of God there are!

As I was turning it over in my mind, the man sudden-ly fell to the ground and lay still. This startled me, and as I had not seen his face, for he had been kneeling with his back to me, I felt curious to go and see who he was. When I got to him I found him in a light sleep. He was a country lad, a young fellow of about twenty-five. He had an attractive face, good-looking, but pale. He was dressed in a peasant's caftan with a bast rope for a girdle. There was nothing else to note about him. He had no *kotomka,*[17] not even a stick. The sound of my approach awoke him and he got up. I asked him who he was, and he told me he was a State peasant of the Smolensk Government and that he was on his way from Kiev. "And where are you going to now?" I asked.

"I don't know myself where God will lead me," he answered.

"Is it long since you left home?"

"Yes, over four years."

"And where have you been living all that time?"

"I have been going from shrine to shrine and to monasteries and churches. There was no point in staying at home. I'm an orphan and I have no relations. Besides, I've got a lame foot. So I'm roaming about the wide world."

"Some God-fearing person, it seems, has taught you not just to roam anywhere, but to visit holy places," said I.

"Well, you see," he answered, "having no father or mother, I used to go about as a boy with the shepherds of our village, and all went happily enough till I was ten years old. Then one day when I had brought the flock home I never noticed that the *starosta's*[18] very best sheep was not among them. And our *starosta* was a bad and inhuman peasant. When he came home that evening and found that his sheep was lost, he rushed at me abusing and threatening. If I didn't go off and find the sheep, he swore he'd beat me to death, and 'I'll break your arms and legs,' he said. Knowing how cruel he was, I went after the sheep, searching the places where they had been feeding in daylight. I searched and searched for more than half the night, but there was not a trace of

---

[17] *Kotomka.* A sort of knapsack made of birch-bark. It has two pockets, one in front and another behind, and is worn slung over the shoulder.

[18] *Starosta.* The head-man of the village community, or *Mir.*

it anywhere. It was such a dark night, too, for it was getting on towards autumn. When I had got very deep into the forest—and in our government the forests are endless—suddenly a storm got up. It was as though the trees were all rocking. In the distance wolves started howling. Such a terror fell upon me that my hair stood on end. What's more, it all got more and more horrible, so that I was ready to drop with fear and horror. Then I fell on my knees and crossed myself, and with all my heart I said: 'Lord Jesus Christ, have mercy on me.' As soon as I had said that I felt absolutely at peace, straight away, as if I had never been in any distress at all. All my fear left me and I felt as happy in my heart as if I had flown away to heaven. This made me very glad, and —well, I just didn't stop saying the Prayer. To this day I don't know whether the storm lasted long and how the night went. I looked up and daylight was coming, and there was I still kneeling in the same place. I got up quietly, I saw I shouldn't find the sheep, and home I went. But all was well in my heart and I was saying the Prayer to my heart's content. As soon as I got to the village the *starosta* saw I hadn't brought the sheep back and thrashed me till I was half dead—he put this foot out of joint, you see. I was laid up, almost unable to move, for six weeks after that beating. All I knew was that I was saying the Prayer and it comforted me. When I got a bit better I began to wander about in the world, and as to be continually jostling about in a crowd didn't interest me, and meant a good deal of sin, I took to roaming from one holy place to another, and in the forests too. That's how I have spent nearly five years now."

When I heard this, my heart was very glad that God had thought me fit to meet so good a man, and I asked him, "And do you often use the Prayer now?"

"I couldn't exist without it," he answered. "Why, if I only just call to mind how I felt that first time in the forest, it's just as if someone pushed me down on my knees and I begin to pray. I don't know whether my sinful prayer is pleasing to God or not. For as I pray, sometimes I feel a great happiness—why, I don't know—a lightness of spirit, a happy sort of quiet; but at other times I feel a dull heaviness and lowness of spirits. But for all that, I want to go on praying always till I die."

"Don't be distressed, dear brother. Everything is pleasing to God and for our slavation—everything, whatever it is that happens in time of prayer. So the holy Fathers say. Whether it's lightness of heart or heaviness, it's all all right. No prayer, good or bad, fails in God's sight. Lightness, warmth and gladness show that God is rewarding and consoling us for the effort, while heaviness, darkness and dryness mean that God is cleansing and strengthening the soul, and by this wholesome trial is saving it, preparing it in humility for the enjoyment of blessed happiness in the future. In proof of this I will read you something that St. John Klimax wrote."

I found the passage and read it to him. He heard it through with care and enjoyed it, and he thanked me very much for it. And so we parted. He went off right into the depth of the forest and I went back to the road. I went on my way, thanking God for treating me, sinner as I am, as fit to be given such teaching.

Next day, by God's help, I came to Kiev. The first and chief thing I wanted was to fast a while and to make my Confession and Communion in that holy town. So I stopped near the saints,[19] as that would be easier for getting to church. A good old Cossack took me in, and as he lived alone in his hut, I found peace and quiet there. At the end of a week, in which I had been getting ready for my Confession, the thought came to me that I would make it as detailed as I could. So I began to recall and go over all my sins from youth onwards very fully, and so as not to forget it all I wrote down everything I could remember in the utmost detail. I covered a large sheet of paper with it.

I heard that at Kitaevaya Pustina, about five miles from Kiev, there was a priest of ascetic life who was very wise and understanding. Whoever went to him for Confession found an atmosphere of tender compassion,

[19] *Near the saints*—*i.e.*, near where they are buried, the Kiev-Pecherskaya Lavra. This was one of the most famous and influential monasteries in Russia and was visited by hundreds of thousands of pilgrims every year. It was founded in the eleventh century, and its catacombs still contain the uncorrupted bodies of many saints of ancient Russia.

and came away with teaching for his salvation and ease of spirit. I was very glad to hear of this and I went to him at once. After I had asked his advice and we had talked awhile, I gave him my sheet of paper to see. He read it through, and then said: "Dear friend, a lot of this that you have written is quite futile. Listen: first, don't bring into Confession sins which you have already repented of and had forgiven. Don't go over them again, for that would be to doubt the power of the sacrament of penance. Next: don't call to mind other people who have been connected with your sins; judge yourself only. Thirdly: the holy Fathers forbid us to mention all the circumstances of the sins, and tell us to acknowledge them in general, so as to avoid temptation both for ourselves and for the priest. Fourthly: you have come to repent and you are not repenting of the fact that you can't repent—*i.e.*, you penitence is lukewarm and careless. Fifthly: you have gone over all these details, but the most important thing you have overlooked: you have not disclosed the gravest sins of all. You have not acknowledged, nor written down, that you do not love God, that you hate your neighbour, that you do not believe in God's Word, and that you are filled with pride and ambition. A whole mass of evil, and all our spiritual depravity is in these four sins. They are the chief roots out of which spring the shoots of all the sins into which we fall."

I was very much surprised to hear this, and I said: "Forgive me, reverend Father, but how is it possible not to love God our Creator and Preserver? What is there to believe in if not the Word of God, in which everything is true and holy? I wish well to all my neighbours, and why should I hate them? I have nothing to be proud of; besides having numberless sins, I have nothing at all which is fit to be praised, and what should I with my poverty and ill-health lust after? Of course, if I were an educated man, or rich, then no doubt I should be guilty of the things you spoke of."

"It's a pity, dear one, that you so little understood what I said. Look! It will teach you more quickly if I give you these notes. They are what I alway use for my own Confession. Read them through, and you will see clearly enough an exact proof of what I said to you just now."

He gave me the notes, and I began to read them, as follows:

"A Confession which Leads the Inward Man to Humility

"Turning my eyes carefully upon myself and watching the course of my inward state, I have verified by experience that I do not love God, that I have no love for my neighbours, that I have no religious belief, and that I am filled with pride and sensuality. All this I actually find in myself as a result of detailed examination of my feelings and conduct, thus:

"1. *I do not love God.* For if I loved God I should be continually thinking about Him with heartfelt joy. Every thought of God would give me gladness and delight. On the contrary, I much more often and much more eagerly think about earthly things, and thinking about God is labour and dryness. If I loved God, then talking with Him in Prayer would be my nourishment and delight and would draw me to unbroken communion with Him. But, on the contrary, I not only find no delight in prayer, but even find it an effort. I struggle with reluctance, I am enfeebled by sloth, and am ready to occupy myself eagerly with my unimportant trifle, if only it shortens prayer and keeps me from it. My time slips away unnoticed in futile occupations, but when I am occupied with God, when I put myself into His presence every hour seems like a year. If one person loves another, he thinks of him throughout the day without ceasing, he pictures him to himself, he cares for him, and in all circumstances his beloved friend is never out of his thoughts. But I, throughout the day, scarcely set aside even a single hour in which to sink deep down into meditation upon God, to inflame my heart with love of Him, while I eagerly give up twenty-three hours as fervent offerings to the idols of my passions. I am forward in talk about frivolous matters and things which degrade the spirit; that gives me pleasure. But in the consideration of God I am dry, bored and lazy. Even if I am unwillingly drawn by others into spiritual conversation, I try to shift the subject quickly to one which pleases my desires. I am tirelessly curious about novelties, about civic affairs and political events; I eagerly seek the satisfaction of my love of knowledge in science and art, and in ways of getting things I want to possess. But the study of the Law of God, the knowledge of God and of religion, make little impression on me, and satisfy no hunger of my soul. I regard these things not only as a non-essential occupation for a Christian, but in a casual way as a sort of side-issue with which I should perhaps occupy my spare time, at odd moments. To put it shortly, if love for God is recognized by the keeping of His commandments (*If ye love Me, keep My commandments,* says our Lord Jesus Christ), and I not only do not keep them, but even make little attempt to do so, then in absolute truth the conclusion follows that I do not love God. That is what Basil the Great says: 'The proof that a man does not love God and His Christ lies in the fact that he does not keep His commandments.'

"2. *I do not love my neighbour either.* For not only am I unable to make up my mind to lay down my life for his sake (according to the Gospel), but I do not even sacrifice my happiness, well-being and peace for the good of my neighbour. If I did love him as myself, as the Gospel bids, his misfortunes would distress me also, his happiness would bring delight to me too. But, on the contrary, I listen to curious, unhappy stories about my neighbour, and I am not distressed; I remain quite undisturbed or, what is still worse, I find a sort of pleasure in them. Bad conduct on the part of my brother I do not cover up with love, but proclaim abroad with censure. His well-being, honour and happiness do not delight me as my own, and, as if they were something quite alien to me, give me no feeling of gladness. What is more, they subtly arouse in me feelings of envy or contempt.

"3. *I have no religious belief.* Neither in immortality nor in the Gospel. If I were firmly persuaded and believed without doubt that beyond the grave lies eternal life and recompense for the deeds of this life, I should be continually thinking of this. The very idea of immortality would terrify me and I should lead this life as a foreigner who gets ready to enter his native land. On the contrary, I do not even think about eternity, and I regard the end of this earthly life as the limit of my existence. The secret thought nestles within me: Who knows what happens at death? If I say I believe in immortality, then I am speaking about my mind only, and my heart is far removed from a firm conviction about it. That is openly witnessed to by conduct and my constant care to satisfy the life of the senses. Were the Holy Gospel taken into my heart in faith, as the Word of God, I should be continually occupied with it, I should study it, find delight in it and with deep devotion fix my attention upon it. Wisdom, mercy, love, are hidden in it; it would lead me to happiness, I should find gladness in the study of the Law of God day and night. In it I should find nourishment like my daily bread and my heart would be drawn to the keeping of its laws. Nothing on earth would be strong enough to turn me away from it. On the contrary, if now and again I read or hear the Word of God, yet even so it is only from necessity or from a general love of knowledge, and approaching it without any very close attention, I find it dull and uninteresting. I usually come to the end of the reading without any profit, only too ready to change over to secular reading in which I take more pleasure and find new and interesting subjects.

"4. *I am full of pride and sensual self-love.* All my actions confirm this. Seeing something good in myself, I want to bring it into view, or to pride myself upon it before other people or inwardly to admire myself for it. Although I display an outward humility, yet I ascribe it all to my own strength and regard myself as superior to others, or at least no worse than they. If I notice a fault in myself, I try to excuse it, I cover it up by saying, 'I am made like that' or 'I am not to blame.' I get angry with those who do not treat me with respect and consider them unable to appreciate the value of people. I brag about my gifts: my failures in any undertaking I regard as a personal insult. I murmur, and I find pleasure in the unhappiness of my enemies. If I strive after anything good it is for the purpose of winning praise, or spiritual self-indulgence, or earthly consolation. In a word, I continually make an idol of myself and render it uninterrupted service, seeking in all things the pleasures of the senses, and nourishment for my sensual passions and lusts.

"Going over all this I see myself as proud, adulterous, unbelieving, without love to God and hating my neighbour. What state could be more sinful? The condition of the spirits of darkness is better than mine. They, although they do not love God, hate men, and live upon pride, yet at least believe and tremble. But I? Can there be a doom more terrible than that which faces me, and what sentence of punishment will be more severe than that upon the careless and foolish life that I recognize in myself?"

On reading through this form of Confession which the priest gave me I was horrified and I thought to myself: "Good Heavens! What frightful sins there are hidden within me and up to now I've never noticed them!" The desire to be cleansed from them made me beg this great spiritual father to teach me how to know the causes of all these evils and how to cure them. And he began to instruct me.

"You see, dear brother, the cause of not loving God is want of belief, want of belief is caused by lack of conviction, and the cause of that is failure to seek for holy and true knowledge, indifference to the light of the spirit. In a word, if you don't believe, you can't love; if you are not convinced, you can't believe, and in order to reach conviction you must get a full and exact knowledge of the matter before you. By meditation, by the study of God's Word and by noting your experience, you must arouse in your soul a thirst and a longing—or, as some call it, 'wonder'—which brings you an insatiable desire to know things more closely and more fully, to go deeper into their nature.

"One spiritual writer speaks of it in this way: 'Love,' he says, 'usually grows with knowledge, and the greater the depth and extent of the knowledge the more love there will be, the more easily the heart will soften and lay itself open to the love of God, as it diligently gazes upon the very fullness and beauty of the divine nature and His unbounded love for men.'

"So now you see that the cause of those sins which you read over is slothfulness in thinking about spiritual things, sloth which stifles the feeling of the need of such thought. If you want to know how to overcome this evil, strive after enlightenment of spirit by every means in your power, attain it by diligent study of the Word of God and of the holy Fathers, by the help of meditation and spiritual counsel and by the conversation of those who are wise in Christ. Ah, dear brother, how much disaster we meet with just because we are lazy about seeking light for our souls through the word of truth. We do not study God's law day and night, and we do not pray about it diligently and unceasingly. And because of this our inner man is hungry and cold, starved, so that it has no strength to take a bold step forward upon the road of righteousness and salvation! And so, beloved, let us resolve to make use of these methods, and as often as possible fill our minds with thoughts of heavenly things; and love, poured down into our hearts from on high, will burst into flame within us. We will do this together and pray as often as we can, for prayer is the chief and strongest means for our renewal and well-being. We will pray, in the words Holy Church teaches us: 'O God, make me fit to love Thee now, as I have loved sin in the past.' "[20]

I listened to all this with care. Deeply moved, I asked this holy father to hear my Confession and to give me Communion. And so next morning after the honour of my Communion, I was for going back to Kiev with this blessed viaticum. But this good father of mine, who was going to the *Lavra*[21] for a couple of days, kept me for that time in his hermit's cell, so that in its silence I might give myself up to prayer without hindrance. And, in fact, I did spend both those days as though I was in

[20] From the eighth prayer in the Morning Prayers of the Lay Prayer Book of the Russian Church.

[21] *Lavra.* Originally a monastery which followed the rule of St. Anthony, but later used simply to designate certain large monasteries. Beside Kiev, there were eight monasteries in Russia which bore the title "Lavra."

heaven. By the prayers of my *starets* I, unworthy as I am, rejoiced in perfect peace. Prayer flowed out in my heart so easily and happily that during that time I think I forgot everthing, and myself; in my mind was Jesus Christ and He alone.

In the end, the priest came back, and I asked his guidance and advice—where should I go now on my pilgrim way? He gave me his blessing with these words, "You go to Pochaev, make your reverence there to the wonder-working Footprint[22] of the most pure Mother of God, and she will guide your feet into the way of peace." And so, taking his advice in faith, three days later I set off for Pochaev.

For some hundred and thirty miles or so I travelled none too happily, for the road lay through pot-houses and Jewish villages and I seldom came across a Christian dwelling. At one farm I noticed a Russian Christian inn and I was glad to see it. I turned in at it to spend the night and also to ask for some bread for my journey, for my rusks were coming to an end. Here I saw the host, an old man with a well-to-do air and who, I learned, came from the same government that I did—the Orlovsky. Directly I went into the room, his first question was: "What religion are you?"

"I replied that I was a Christian, and *pravoslavny*.[23] "*Pravoslavny,* indeed," said he with a laugh. "You people are *pravoslavny* only in word—in act you are heathen. I know all about your religion, brother. A learned priest once tempted me and I tried it. I joined your Church, and stayed in it for six months. After that I came back to the ways of our society. To join your

---

[22] *The Holy Footprint*. The legend, which is said to date from about the thirteenth century, says that Our Lady surrounded by saints appeared in a blaze of glory to a group of shepherds. The rock upon which she stood was afterwards found to bear the imprint of her foot, and from it trickled a flow of water which subsequently proved to have healing powers. A monastery was later built over the site and the shrine of the Footprint is still preserved in the crypt.

[23] *Pravoslavny*. The name which the Russians give to the Orthodox Church. Literally it means "right praising."

Church is just a snare. The readers mumble the service all anyhow, with things missed out and things you can't understand. And the singing is no better than you hear in a pub. And the people stand all in a huddle, men and women all mixed up; they talk while the service is going on, turn round and stare about, walk to and fro and give you no peace and quiet to say your prayers. What sort of worship do you call that? It's just a sin! Now, with us how devout the service is; you can hear what's said, nothing is missed out, the singing is most moving and the people stand quietly, the men by themselves, the women by themselves, and everybody knows what reverence to make and when, as Holy Church directs. Really and truly, when you come into a church of ours, you feel you have come to the worship of God; but in one of yours you can't imagine what you've come to—to Church or to market!"

From all this I saw that the old man was a diehard *raskolnik*.[24] But he spoke so plausibly, I could not argue with him nor convert him. I just thought to myself that it will be impossible to convert the Old Believers to the true Church until church services are put right among us and until the clergy in particular set an example in this. The *raskolnik* knows nothing of the inner life; he relies upon externals, and it is about them that we are careless.

[24] *Raskolniki*. Literally "schismatics", sometimes called Old Believers. In the seventeenth century Nikon, the Patriarch of Moscow, in the face of fierce opposition, carried through a reform of the Service Books. The Old Believers, led by Avvakum, seceded from the Church rather than accept the changes. The origin of Russian Dissent is, therefore, the exact opposite of the origin of English Dissent. The *Raskolniki* afterwards themselves split into more sects, some having a priesthood and some being without. Some of these sects degenerated into oddities, and indulged in the strangest excesses. But the more sober element among the Old Believers incorporates some of the best of the Russian religious spirit and character. Altogether these sects numbered some two per cent of the Christian population of the Empire at the beginning of the twentieth century. There is an English version of the autobiography of the archpriest Avvakum.

So I wanted to get away from here and had already gone out into the hall when to my surprise I saw through the open door of a private room a man who did not look like a Russian; he was lying on a bed and reading a book. He beckoned me and asked me who I was. I told him. And then he began: "Listen, dear friend. Won't you agree to look after a sick man, say for a week, until by God's help I get better? I am a Greek, a monk from Mount Athos. I'm in Russia to collect alms for my monastery and on my way back I've fallen ill, so that I can't walk for the pain in my legs. So I've taken this room here. Don't say no, servant of God! I'll pay you."

"There is no need whatever to pay me. I will very gladly look after you as best I can in the name of God." So I stayed with him. I heard a great deal from him about the things which concern the salvation of our souls. He told me about Athos, the Holy Mountain, about the great *podvizhniki*[25] there, and about the many hermits and anchorites. He had with him a copy of *The Philokalia* in Greek, and a book by Isaac the Syrian. We read together and compared the Slavonic translation by Paisy Velichovsky with the Greek original. He declared that it would be impossible to translate from Greek more accurately and faithfully than *The Philokalia* had been turned into Slavonic by Paisy.

As I noticed that he was always in prayer and versed in the inward prayer of the heart, and as he spoke Russian perfectly, I questioned him on this matter. He readily told me a great deal about it and I listened with care. I even wrote down many things that he said. Thus, for example, he taught me about the excellence and greatness of the Jesus Prayer in this way. "Even the very form of the Jesus Prayer," he said, "shows what a great prayer it is. It is made up of two parts. In the first, *i.e.,* 'Lord Jesus Christ, Son of God,' it leads our thoughts to the life of Jesus Christ, or, as the holy Fathers put it, it is the whole Gospel in brief. In the second part, 'Have

[25] *Podvizhnik.* A *podvig* is a notable exploit, and the man who performs it is a *podvizhnik.* The terms are applied in the spiritual life to outstanding achievements in the life of prayer and ascetic practices, and to those who attain to them.

mercy on me, a sinner,' it faces us with the story of our own helplessness and sinfulness. And it is to be noted that the desire and petition of a poor, sinful, humble soul could not be put into words more wise, more clear cut, more exact than these—'have mercy on me.' No other form of words would be as satisfying and full as this. For instance, if one said, 'Forgive me, put away my sins, cleanse my transgressions, blot out my offences,' all that would express one petition only—asking to be set free from punishment, the fear of a faint-hearted and listless soul. But to say 'Have mercy on me' means not only the desire for pardon arising from fear, but is the sincere cry of filial love, which puts its hope in the mercy of God and humbly acknowledges it is too weak to break its own will and to keep a watchful guard over itself. It is a cry for mercy—that is, for grace—which will show itself in the gift of strength from God, to enable us to resist temptation and overcome our sinful inclinations. It is like a penniless debtor asking his kindly creditor not only to forgive him the debt but also to pity his extreme poverty and to give him alms—that is what these profound words 'have mercy on me' express. It is like saying: 'Gracious Lord, forgive me my sins and help me to put myself right; arouse in my soul a strong impulse to follow Thy bidding. Bestow Thy grace in forgiving my actual sins and in turning my heedless mind, will and heart to Thee alone.' "

Upon this I wondered at the wisdom of his words and thanked him for teaching my sinful soul, and he went on teaching me other wonderful things.

"If you like," said he (and I took him to be something of a scholar, for he said he had studied at the Athens Academy), "I will go on and tell you about the tone in which the Jesus Prayer is said. I happen to have heard many God-fearing Christian people say the oral Jesus Prayer as the Word of God bids them and according to the tradition of Holy Church. They use it so both in their private prayers and in church. If you listen carefully and as a friend to this quiet saying of the Prayer, you can notice for your spiritual profit that the tone of the praying voice varies with different people. Thus, some stress the very first word of the Prayer and say *Lord* Jesus Christ, and then finish all the other words on one level tone. Others begin the Prayer in a level voice and throw the stress in the middle of the Prayer, on the word *Jesus* as an exclamation, and the rest, again, they finish in an unstressed tone, as they began. Others, again, begin and go on with the Prayer without stress until they come to the last words—*Have mercy on me*—when they raise their voices in ecstasy. And some say the whole Prayer—Lord Jesus Christ, Son of God, have mercy on me a sinner—with all the stress upon the single phrase—*Son of God*.

"Now listen. The Prayer is one and the same. Orthodox Christians hold one and the same profession of faith. The knowledge is common to all of them, that this sublime Prayer of all prayers includes two things: the Lord Jesus and the appeal to Him. That is known to be the same for everybody. Why then do they not all express it in the same way, why not all in the same tone, that is? Why does the soul plead specially, and express itself with particular stress, not in one and the same place for all, but in a certain place for each? Many say of this that perhaps it is the result of habit, or of copying other people, or that it depends upon a way of understanding the words which corresponds with the individual point of view, or finally that it is just as it comes most easily and naturally to each person. But I think quite differently about it. I should like to look for something higher in it, something unknown not only to the listener, but even to the person who is praying also. May there not be here a hidden moving of the Holy Spirit *making intercession for us with groanings which cannot be uttered* in those who do not know how and about what to pray? And if everyone prays in the Name of Jesus Christ, by the Holy Spirit, as the Apostle says, the Holy Spirit, who works in secret and gives a prayer to him who prays, may also bestow His beneficent gift upon all, notwithstanding their lack of strength. To one He may give the reverent fear of God, to another love, to another firmness of faith, and to another gracious humility, and so on.

"If this be so, then he who has been given the gift of revering and praising the power of the Almighty will in his prayers stress with special feeling the word *Lord* in which he feels the greatness and the might of the Creator of the world. He who has been given the secret outpouring of love in his heart is thrown into rapture and filled with gladness as he exclaims *Jesus Christ,* just as a certain *starets* could not hear the Name of Jesus without a peculiar flood of love and gladness, even in ordinary conversation. The unshakable believer in the Godhead of Jesus Christ, of one Substance with the Father, is enkindled with still more fervent faith as he says the words *Son of God.* One who has received the gift of humility and is deeply aware of his own weakness, with the words *have mercy on me* is penitent and humbled, and pours out his heart most richly in these last words of the Jesus Prayer. He cherishes hope in the loving kindness of God and abhors his own falling into sin. There you have the causes, in my opinion, of the differing tones in which people say the Prayer in the Name of Jesus. And from this you may note as you listen, to the glory of God and your own instruction, by what emotion any one is specially moved, what spiritual gift any one person has. A number of people have said to me on this subject: 'Why do not all these signs of hidden spiritual gifts appear together and united? Then not only one, but every word of the Prayer would be imbued with one and the same tone of rapture.' I have answered in this way: 'Since the grace of God distributes His gift in wisdom to every man severally according to his strength, as we see from Holy Scripture, who can search out with his finite mind and enter into the dispositions of grace? Is not the clay completely in the power of the potter, and is he not able to make one thing or another out of the clay?' "

I spent five days with this *starets*, and he began to get very much better in health. This time was of so much profit to me that I did not notice how quickly it went. For in that little room, in silent seclusion, we were concerned with nothing else whatever than silent prayer in the Name of Jesus, or talk about the same subject, interior prayer.

One day a pilgrim came to see us. He complained bitterly about the Jews and abused them. He had been going about their villages and had to put up with their unfriendliness and cheating. He was so bitter against them that he cursed them, even saying they were not fit to live because of their obstinacy and unbelief. Finally he said that he had such an aversion for them that it was quite beyond his control.

"You have no right, friend," said the *starets,* "to abuse and curse the Jews like this. God made them just as He made us. You should be sorry for them and pray for them not curse them. Believe me, the disgust you feel for them comes from the fact that you are not grounded in the love of God and have no interior prayer as a security and, therefore, no inward peace. I will read you a passage from the holy Fathers about this. Listen, this is what Mark the Podvizhnik writes: 'The soul which is inwardly united to God becomes, in the greatness of its joy, like a good-natured simple-hearted child, and now condemns no one, Greek, heathen, Jew nor sinner, but looks at them all alike with sight that has been cleansed, finds joy in the whole world, and wants everybody—Greeks and Jews and heathen—to praise God.' And Macarius the Great, of Egypt, says that the inward contemplative 'burns with so great a love that if it were possible he would have everyone to dwell within him, making no difference between bad and good.' There, dear brother, you see what the holy Fathers think about it. So I advise you to lay aside your fierceness, and look upon everything as under the all-knowing providence of God, and when you meet with vexations accuse yourself especially of lack of patience and humility.

At last more than a week went by and my *starets* got well, and I thanked him from my heart for all the blessed instruction that he had given me, and we said good-bye. He set off for home and I started upon the way I had planned. Now I began to get near to Pochaev. I had not gone more than seventy miles when a soldier overtook me and I asked him where he was going. He told me he was going back to his native district in Kamenets Podolsk. We went along in silence for seven miles or so, and I noticed that he sighed very heavily as though something was distressing him, and he was very gloomy. I asked him why he was so sad.

"Good friend, if you have noticed my sorrow and will swear by all you hold sacred never to tell anybody, I will tell you all about myself, for I am near to death and I have no one to talk to about it."

I assured him, as a Christian, that I had not the slightest need to tell anybody about it, and that out of brotherly love I should be glad to give him any advice that I could.

"Well, you see," he began, "I was drafted as a soldier from the State Peasants. After about five years' service it became intolerably hard for me; in fact, they often flogged me for negligence and for drunkenness. I took it into my head to run away, and here I am a deserter for the last fifteen years. For six years I hid wherever I could. I stole from farms and larders and warehouses. I stole horses. I broke into shops and followed this sort of trade, always on my own. I got rid of my stolen goods in various ways. I drank the money, I led a depraved life, committed every sin. Only my soul didn't perish. I got on very well, but in the end I got into gaol for wandering without a passport. But when a chance came I even escaped from there. Then unexcectedly I met with a soldier who had been discharged from the service and was going home to a distant government; and as he was ill and could hardly walk he asked me to take him to the nearest village where he could find a lodging. So I took him. The police allowed us to spend the night in a barn on some hay and there we lay down. When I woke up in the morning I glanced at my soldier and there he was dead and stiff. Well, I hurriedly searched for his passport—that is to say, his discharge—and when I found it and a fair amount of money too, while everybody was still asleep, I was out of that shed and the back yard as quickly as I could and so into the forest, and off I went. On reading his passport I saw that in age and distinguishing marks he was almost the same as I. I was very glad about this and went on boldly into the depths of the Astrakhan Government. There I began to steady down a bit and I got a job as a labourer. I joined up with an old man there who had his own house and was a cattle dealer. He lived alone with his daughter, who was a widow. When I had lived with him for a year I married this daughter of his. Then the old man died. We could not carry on the business. I started drinking again, and my wife too, and in a year we had got through everything the old man had left. And then my wife took ill and died. So I sold everything that was left, and the house, and I soon ran through the money.

"Now I had nothing to live on, nothing to eat. So I went back to my old trade of dealing in stolen goods, and all the more boldly now because I had a passport. So I took to my old evil life again for about a year. There came a time when for a long while I met with no success. I stole an old wretched horse from a *bobil*[26] and I sold it to the knackers for a bob. Taking the money, I went off to a pub and began to drink. I had an idea of going to a village where there was a wedding, and while everybody was asleep after the feasting I meant to pick up whatever I could. As the sun had not yet set I went into the forest to wait for night. I lay down there and fell into a deep sleep. Then I had a dream and saw myself standing in a wide and beautiful meadow. Suddenly a terrible cloud began to rise in the sky, and then there came such a terrific clap of thunder that the ground trembled underneath me and it was as though someone drove me up to my shoulders into the ground which jammed against me on all sides. Only my head and my hands were left outside. Then this terrible cloud seemed to come down on to the ground and out of it came my grandfather, who had been dead for twenty years. He was a very upright man and for thirty years was a churchwarden in our village. With an angry and threatening face he came up to me and I shook with fear. Round about nearby I saw several heaps of things which I had stolen at various times. I was still more frightened. My grandfather came up to me and, pointing to the first heap, said threateningly: 'What is that? Let him have it!' And suddenly the ground on all sides of me began to squeeze me so hard that I could not bear the pain and the faintness. I groaned and cried out, 'Have mercy on me,' but the torment went on. Then my grandfather

[26] *Bobil.* A landless peasant, hence a miserable poverty-stricken fellow.

pointed to another heap and said again: 'What is that? Crush him harder!' And I felt such violent pain and agony that no torture on earth could compare with it. Finally, that grandfather of mine brought near me the horse that I had stolen the evening before, and cried out: 'And what is this? Let him have it as hard as you can.' And I got such pain from all sides that I can't describe it; it was so cruel, terrible and exhausting. It was as though all my sinews were being drawn out of me and I was suffocated by the frightful pain. I felt I could not bear it and that I should collapse unconscious if that torture went on even a little bit longer. But the horse kicked out and caught me on the cheek and cut it open, and the moment I got that blow I woke up in utter horror and shaking like a weakling. I saw that it was already daylight, the sun was rising. I touched my cheek and blood was flowing from it; and those parts of me which in my dream had been in the ground were all, so to say, hard and stiff and I had pins and needles in them. I was in such terror that I could hardly get up and go home. My cheek hurt for a long time. Look, you can see the scar now. It wasn't there before. And so, after this, fear and horror often used to come over me and now I only have to remember what I suffered in that dream for the agony and exhaustion to begin again and such torture that I don't know what to do with myself. What is more, it began to come more often, and in the end I began to be afraid of people and to feel ashamed as though everybody knew my past dishonesty. Then I could neither eat nor drink nor sleep because of this suffering. I was worn to a ravel. I did think of going to my regiment and making a clean breast of everything. Perhaps God would forgive my sins if I took my punishment. But I was afraid and I lost my courage because they would make me run the gauntlet. And so, losing patience, I wanted to hang myself. But the thought came to me that in any case I shan't live for a very long time; I shall soon die, for I have lost all my strength. And so I thought I would go and say good-bye to my home and die there. I have a nephew at home. And here I am on my way there for six months now. And all the while grief and fear make me miserable. What do you think, my friend? What am I to do? I really can't bear much more."

When I heard all this I was astonished and I praised the wisdom and the goodness of God, as I saw the different ways in which they are brought to sinners. So I said to him: "Dear brother, during the time of that fear and agony you ought to have prayed to God. That is the great cure for all our troubles."

"Not on your life!" he said to me. "I thought that directly I began to pray God would destroy me."

"Nonsense, brother; it is the Devil puts thoughts like that into your head. There is no end to God's mercy and He is sorry for sinners and quickly forgives all who repent. Perhaps you don't know the Jesus Prayer: 'Lord Jesus Christ, have mercy on me, a sinner.' You go on saying that without stopping."

"Why, of course I know that Prayer. I used to say it sometimes to keep my courage up when I was going to do a robbery."

"Now, look here. God did not destroy you when you were on your way to do something wrong and said the Prayer. Will He do so when you start praying on the path of repentance? Now, you see how your thoughts come from the Devil. Believe me, dear brother, if you will say that Prayer, taking no notice of whatever thoughts come into your mind, then you will quickly feel relief. All the fear and strain will go and in the end you will be completely at peace. You will become a devout man and all sinful passions will leave you. I assure you of this, for I have seen a great deal of it in my time."

After that I told him about several cases in which the Jesus Prayer had shown its wonderful power to work upon sinners. In the end I persuaded him to come with me to the Pochaev Mother of God, the refuge of sinners, before he went home, and to make his Confession and Communion there.

My soldier listened to all this attentively and, as I could see, with joy, and he agreed to everything. We went to Pochaev together on this condition, that neither of us should speak to the other, but that we should say the Jesus Prayer all the time. In this silence we walked for a whole day. Next day he told me that he felt much

easier and it was plain that his mind was calmer than
before. On the third day we arrived at Pochaev and I
urged him again not to break off the Prayer either day
or night while he was awake, and assured him that the
most Holy Name of Jesus, which is unbearable to our
spiritual foes, would be strong to save him. On this point
I read to him from *The Philokalia,* that although we
ought to say the Jesus Prayer at all times, it is especially
needful to do so with the utmost care when we are preparing for Communion.

So he did, and then he made his Confession and
Communion. Although from time to time the old
thoughts still came over him, yet he easily drove them
away with the Jesus Prayer. On Sunday, so as to be up
for Mattins more easily, he went to bed earlier and went
on saying the Jesus Prayer. I still sat in the corner and
read my *Philokalia* by a rushlight. An hour went past;
he fell asleep and I set myself to prayer. All of a sudden,
about twenty minutes later, he gave a start and woke up,
jumped quickly out of bed, ran over to me in tears and,
speaking with the greatest happiness, he said: "Oh,
brother, what I have just seen! How peaceful and happy
I am; I believe that God has mercy upon sinners, and
does not torment them. Glory to Thee, O Lord, Glory to
Thee."

I was surprised and glad and asked him to tell me exactly what had happened to him.

"Why, this," he said. "Directly I fell asleep I saw myself in that meadow where they tortured me. At first I
was terrified, but I saw that, instead of a cloud, the
bright sun was rising and a wonderful light shining over
the whole meadow. And I saw red flowers and grass in
it. Then suddenly my grandfather came up to me, looking nicer than you ever saw, and he greeted me gently
and kindly. And he said: 'Go to Zhitomir, to the Church
of St. George. They will take you under church protection. Spend the rest of your life there and pray without
ceasing. God will be gracious to you.' When he said this
he made the sign of the cross over me and straight away
vanished. I can't tell you how happy I felt; it was as
though a load had been taken off my shoulders and I
had flown away to heaven. At that point I woke up, feel-

ing easy in my mind and my heart so full of joy that I
didn't know what to do. What ought I to do now? I shall
start straight away for Zhitomir, as my grandfather told
me. I shall find it easy going with the Prayer."

"But wait a minute, dear brother. How can you start
off in the middle of the night? Stay for Mattins, say
your prayers and then start off with God."

So we didn't go to sleep after this conversation. We
went to church; he stayed all through Mattins, praying
earnestly with tears, and he said that he felt very peaceful and glad and that the Jesus Prayer was going on happily. Then after the Liturgy he made his Communion
and when we had had some food I went with him as far
as the Zhitomir road, where we said good-bye with tears
of gladness.

After this I began to think about my own affairs.
Where should I go now? In the end I decided that I
would go back again to Kiev. The wise teaching of my
priest there drew me that way, and, besides, if I stayed
with him he might find some Christ-loving philanthropist
who would put me on my way to Jerusalem or at least to
Mount Athos. So I stopped another week at Pochaev,
spending the time in recalling all I had learned from
those I had met on this journey and in making notes of a
number of helpful things. Then I got ready for the journey, put on my *kotomka* and went to church to com-
mend my journey to the Mother of God. When the Liturgy was over I said my prayers and was ready to start.
I was standing at the back of the church when a man
came in, not very richly dressed, but clearly one of the
gentry, and he asked me where the candles were sold. I
showed him. At the end of the Liturgy I stayed praying
at the shrine of the Footprint. When I had finished my
prayers I set off on my way. I had gone a little way
along the street when I saw an open window in one of
the houses at which a man sat reading a book. My way
took me past that very window and I saw that the man
sitting there was the same one who had asked me about
the candles in church. As I went by I took off my hat,
and when he saw me he beckoned me to come to him,
and said: "I suppose you must be a pilgrim?"

"Yes," I answered.

He asked me in and wanted to know who I was and where I was going. I told him all about myself and hid nothing. He gave me some tea and began to talk to me.

"Listen, my little pigeon; I should advise you to go to the *Solovetsky*[27] Monastery. There is a very secluded and peaceful *skeet*[28] there called *Anzersky*. It is like a second Athos and they welcome everybody there. The novitiate consists only in this: that they take turns to read the psalter in church four hours out of the twenty-four. I am going there myself and I have taken a vow to go on foot. We might go together. I should be safer with you; they say it is a very lonely road. On the other hand, I have got money and I could supply you with food the whole way. And I should propose we went on these terms, that we walked half a dozen yards apart; then we should not be in each other's way, and as we went we could spend the time in reading all the while or in meditation. Think it over, brother, and do agree; it will be worth your while."

When I heard this invitation I took this unexpected event as a sign for my journey from the Mother of God whom I had asked to teach me the way to blessedness. And without further thought I agreed at once. And so we set out the next day. We walked for three days, as we had agreed, one behind the other. He read a book the whole time, a book which never left his hand day or night; and at times he was meditating about something. At last we came to a halt at a certain place for dinner. He ate his food with the book lying open in front of him and he was continually looking at it. I saw that the book was a copy of the Gospels, and I said to him: "May I venture to ask, sir, why you never allow the Gospels out of your hand day or night? Why you always hold it and carry it with you?"

"Because," he answered, "from it and it alone I am almost continually learning."

[27] *Solovetsky*. The famous monastery on the group of islands of that name in the White Sea. It was founded in 1429 by St. German and St. Sabbas. The former had been a monk of Valaam.

[28] A *Skeet* is a small monastic community dependent upon a large monastery.

"And what are you learning?" I went on.

"The Christian life, which is summed up in prayer. I consider that prayer is the most important and necessary means of salvation and the first duty of every Christian. Prayer is the first step in the devout life and also its crown, and that is why the Gospel bids unceasing prayer. To other acts of piety their own times are assigned, but in the matter of prayer there are no off times. Without prayer it is impossible to do any good and without the Gospel you cannot learn properly about prayer. Therefore, all those who have reached salvation by way of the interior life, the holy preachers of the Word of God, as well as hermits and recluses, and indeed all God-fearing Christians, were taught by their unfailing and constant occupation with the depths of God's Word and by reading the Gospel. Many of them had the Gospel constantly in their hands, and in their teaching about salvation gave the advice: 'Sit down in the silence of your cell and read the Gospel and read it again.' There you have the reason why I concern myself with the Gospel alone."

I was very much pleased with this reasoning of his and with his eagerness for prayer. I went on to ask him from which Gospel in particular he got the teaching about prayer. "From all four Evangelists," he answered; "in a word, from the whole of the New Testament, reading it in order. I have been reading it for a long time and taking in the meaning, and it has shown me that there is a graduation and a regular chain of teaching about prayer in the holy Gospel, beginning from the first Evangelist and going right through in a regular order, in a system. For instance, at the very beginning there is laid down the approach, or the introduction to teaching about prayer; then the form or the outward expression of it in words. Farther on we have the necessary conditions upon which prayer may be offered, the means of learning it, and examples; and finally the secret teaching about interior and spiritual ceaseless prayer in the Name of Jesus Christ, which is set forth as higher and more salutary than formal prayer. And then comes its necessity, its blessed fruit, and so on. In a word, there is to be found in the Gospel full and detailed knowledge about

prayer, in systematic order or sequence
ing to end."

I heard this I decided to ask him to show me
is in detail. So I said: "As I like hearing and talking about prayer more than anything else, I should be
very glad indeed to see this secret chain of teaching
about prayer in all its details. For the love of God, then,
show me all this in the Gospel itself."

He readily agreed to this and said: "Open your Gospel; look at it and make notes about what I say." And
he gave me a pencil. "Be so good as to look at these
notes of mine. Now," said he, "look out first of all in the
Gospel of St. Matthew the sixth chapter and read from
the fifth to the ninth verses. You see that here we have
the preparation or the introduction, teaching that not for
vainglory and noisily, but in a solitary place and in quietude, we should begin our prayer, and pray only for for-
giveness of sins and for communion with God, and not
devising many and unnecessary petitions about various
worldly things as the heathen do. Then, read farther on
in the same chapter, from the ninth to the fourteenth
verses. Here the form of prayer is given to us—that is to
say, in what sort of words it ought to be expressed.
There you have brought together in great wisdom everything that is necessary and desirable for our life. After
that, go on and read the fourteenth and fifteenth verses
of the same chapter, and you will see the conditions it is
necessary to observe so that prayer may be effective.
For unless we forgive those who have injured us, God
will not forgive our sins. Pass on now to the seventh
chapter, and you will find in the seventh to the twelfth
verses how to succeed in prayer, to be bold in hope—
ask, seek, knock. These strong expressions depict frequency in prayer and the urgency of practising it, so that
prayer shall not only accompany all actions but even
come before them in time. This constitutes the principal
property of prayer. You will see an example of this in
the fourteenth chapter of St. Mark and the thirty-second
to the fortieth verses, where Jesus Christ Himself repeats
the same words of prayer frequently. St. Luke, chapter
eleven, verses five to fourteen, gives a similar example
of repeated prayer in the Parable of the Friend at Mid-

night and the repeated request of the Importunate Widow (St. Luke xviii. 1–8), illustrating the command of Jesus Christ that we should pray always, at all times and in every place, and not grow discouraged—that is to say, not get lazy. After this detailed teaching we have shown to us in the Gospel of St. John the essential teaching about the secret interior prayer of the heart. In the first place we are shown it in the profound story of the conversation of Jesus Christ with the woman of Samaria, in which is revealed the interior worship of God *in spirit and in truth* which God desires and which is unceasing true prayer, like living water flowing into eternal life (St. John iv. 5–25). Farther on, in the fifteenth chapter, verses four to eight, there is pictured for us still more decidedly the power and the might and the necessity of inward prayer—that is to say, of the presence of the spirit in Christ in unceasing remembrance of God. Finally, read verses twenty-three to twenty-five in the sixteenth chapter of the same Evangelist. See what a mystery is revealed here. You notice that prayer in the Name of Jesus Christ, or what is known as the Jesus Prayer—that is to say, 'Lord Jesus Christ, have mercy on me'—when frequently repeated, had the greatest power and very easily opens the heart and blesses it. This is to be noticed very clearly in the case of the Apostles, who had been for a whole year disciples of Jesus Christ, and had already been taught the Lord's Prayer by Him—that is to say, 'Our Father' (and it is through them that we know it). Yet at the end of His earthly life Jesus Christ revealed to them the mystery which was still lacking in their prayers. So that their prayer might make a definite step forward He said to them: *Hitherto have ye asked nothing in My Name. Verily I say unto you, Whatsoever ye shall ask the Father in My Name He will give it you.* And so it happened in their case. For, ever after this time, when the Apostles learned to offer prayers in the Name of Jesus Christ, how many wonderful works they performed and what abundant light was shed upon them. Now, do you see the chain, the fullness of teaching about prayer deposited with such wisdom in the Holy Gospel? And if you go on after this to the reading of the Apostolic Epistles, in them also you can find the same successive teaching about prayer.

"To continue the notes I have already given you I will show you several places which illustrate the properties of prayer. Thus, in the Acts of the Apostles the practice of it is described—that is to say, the diligent and constant exercise of prayer by the first Christians, who were enlightened by their faith in Jesus Christ (Acts iv. 31). The fruits of prayer are told us, or the results of being constantly in prayer—that is to say, the outpouring of the Holy Spirit and His gifts upon those who pray. You will see something similar to this in the sixteenth chapter, verses twenty-five and twenty-six. Then follow it up in order in the Apostolic Epistles and you will see (1) how necessary prayer is in all circumstances (Jas. v. 13–16); (2) how the Holy Spirit helps us to pray (Jude 20–21 and Rom. viii. 26); (3) how we ought all to pray in the spirit (Eph. vi. 18); (4) how necessary calm and inward peace are to prayer (Phil. iv. 6, 7); (5) how necessary it is to pray without ceasing (1 Thess. v. 17); (6) and finally we notice that one ought to pray not only for oneself but also for all men (1 Tim. ii. 1–5). Thus, by spending a long time with great care in drawing out the meaning we can find many more revelations still of secret knowledge hidden in the Word of God, which escape one if one reads it but rarely or hurriedly.

"Do you notice, after what I have now shown you, with what wisdom and how systematically the New Testament reveals the teaching of our Lord Jesus Christ on this matter which we have been tracing? In what a wonderful sequence it is put in all four Evangelists? It is like this. In St. Matthew we see the approach, the introduction to prayer, the actual form of prayer, conditions of it, and so on. Go farther. In St. Mark we find examples. In St. Luke, parables. In St. John, the secret exercise of inward prayer, although this is also found in all four Evangelists, either briefly or at length. In the Acts the practice of prayer and the results of prayer are pictured for us; in the Apostolic Epistles, and in the Apocalypse itself, many properties inseparably connected with the act of prayer. And there you have the reason that I am content with the Gospels alone as my teacher in all the ways of salvation."

All the while he was showing me this and teaching me I marked in the Gospels (in my Bible) all the places which he pointed out to me. It seemed to me most remarkable and instructive, and I thanked him very much.

Then we went on for another five days in silence. My fellow-pilgrim's feet began to hurt him very much, no doubt because he was not used to continuous walking. So he hired a cart with a pair of horses and took me with him. And so we have come into your neighbourhood and have stayed here for three days, so that when we have had some rest we can set off straight away to Anzersky, where he is so anxious to go.

The Starets. This friend of yours is splendid. Judging from his piety he must be very well instructed. I should like to see him.

The Pilgrim. We are stopping in the same place. Let me bring him to you tomorrow. It is late now. Goodbye.

6

THE PILGRIM. As I promised when I saw you yesterday, I have asked my revered fellow-pilgrim, who solaced my pilgrim way with spiritual conversation and whom you wanted to see, to come here with me.

The Starets. It will be very nice both for me and, I hope, also for these revered visitors of mine, to see you both and to have the advantage of hearing your experiences. I have with me here a venerable skhimnik, and here a devout priest. And so, where two or three are gathered together in the Name of Jesus Christ, there He promised to be Himself. And now, here are five of us in His Name, and so no doubt He will vouchsafe to bless us all the more bountifully. The story which your fellow pilgrim told me yesterday, dear . brother, about your burning attachment to the Holy Gospel is most notable and instructive. It would be interesting to know in what way this great and blessed secret was revealed to you.

The Professor. The all-loving God, who desires that all men should be saved and come to the knowledge of the truth, revealed it to me of His great loving kindness in a marvellous way, without any human intervention. For five years I was a professor and I led a gloomy dissipated sort of life, captivated by the vain philosophy of the world, and not according to Christ. Perhaps I should have perished altogether had I not been upheld to some extent by the fact that I lived with my very devout mother and my sister, who was a serious-minded young woman. One day, when I was taking a walk along the public boulevard, I met and made the acquaintance of an excellent young man who told me he was a Frenchman, a student who had not long ago arrived from Paris and was looking for a post as tutor. His high degree of culture delighted me very much, and he being a stranger in this country I asked him to my home and we became friends. In the course of two months he frequently came to see me. Sometimes we went for walks together and amused ourselves, and went together into company which I leave you to suppose was very immoral. At length he came to me one day with an invitation to a place of that sort; and in order to persuade me more quickly he began to praise the particular liveliness and pleasantness of the company to which he was inviting me. After he had been speaking about it for a short while, suddenly he began to ask me to come with him out of my study where we were sitting and to sit in the drawing-room. This seemed to me very odd. So I said that I had never before noticed any reluctance on his part to be in my study, and what, I asked, was the cause of it now? And I added that the drawing-room was next door to the room where my mother and sister were, and for us to carry on this sort of conversation there would be unseemly. He pressed his point on various pretexts, and finally came out quite openly with this: "Among those books on your shelves there you have a copy of the Gospels. I have such a reverence for that book that in its presence I find a difficulty in talking about our disreputable affairs. Please take it away from here; then we can talk freely." In my frivolous way I smiled at his words. Taking the Gospels from the shelf I said, "You ought to have told me that long ago," and handed it to him, saying, "Well, take it yourself and put it down somewhere in the room." No sooner had I touched him with the Gospels than at that instant he trembled and *disappeared*. This dumbfounded me to such an extent that I fell senseless to the floor with fright. Hearing the noise, my household came running in to me and for a full half-hour they were unable to bring me to my senses. In the end, when I came to myself again, I was frightened and shaky and I felt thoroughly upset, and my hands and my feet were absolutely numb so that I could not move them. When the doctor was called in he diagnosed paralysis as the result of some great shock or fright. I was laid up for a whole year after this, and with the most careful medical attention from many doctors I did not get the smallest alleviation, so that as a result of my illness it looked as though I should have to resign my position. My mother, who was growing old, died during this period and my sister was preparing to take the veil, and all this increased my illness all the more. I had but one consolation during this time of sickness, and that was reading the Gospel, which from the beginning of my illness never left my hands. It was a sort of pledge of the marvellous thing that had happened to me. One day an unknown recluse came to see me. He was making a collection for his monastery. He spoke to me very persuasively and told me that I should not rely only upon medicines, which without the help of God were unable to bring me relief, and that I should pray to God and pray diligently about this very thing, for prayer is the most powerful means of healing all sicknesses both bodily and spiritual.

"How can I pray in such a position as this, when I have not the strength to make any sort of reverence, nor can I lift my hands to cross myself?" I answered in my bewilderment. To this he said, "Well, at any rate, pray somehow." But farther he did not go, nor actually explain to me how to pray. When my visitor left me I seemed almost involuntarily to start thinking about prayer and about its power and its effects, calling to mind the instruction I had had in religious knowledge long ago when I was still a student. This occupied me very happily and renewed in my mind my knowledge of religious matters, and it warmed my heart. At the same time I began to feel a certain relief in my attack of illness. Since the book of the Gospels was continually with me, such was my faith in it as the result of the miracle; and as I remembered also that the whole discourse upon prayer which I had heard in lectures was based upon the Gospel text, I considered that the best thing would be to make a study of prayer and Christian devotion solely upon the teaching of the Gospel. Working out its meaning, I drew upon it as from an abundant spring, and found a complete system of the life of salvation and of true interior prayer. I reverently marked all the passages on this subject, and from that time I have been trying zealously to learn this divine teaching, and with all my might, though not without difficulty, to put it into practice. While I was occupied in this way my health gradually improved, and in the end, as you see, I recovered completely. As I was still living alone I decided in thankfulness to God for His fatherly kindness, which had given me recovery of health and enlightenment of mind, to follow the example of my sister and the prompting of my own heart, and to dedicate myself to the solitary life, so that unhindered I might receive and make my own those sweet words of eternal life given me in the Word of God. So here I am at the present time, stealing off to the solitary *skeet* in the Solovetsky Monastery in the White Sea, which is called Anzersky, about which I have heard on good authority that it is a most suitable place for the contemplative life. Further I will tell you this. The Holy Gospel gives me much consolation in this journey of mine, and sheds abundant light upon my untutored mind, and warms my chilly heart. Yet the fact is that in spite of all I frankly acknowledge my weakness, and I freely admit that the conditions of fulfilling the work of devotion and attaining salvation, the requirement of thoroughgoing self-denial, of extraordinary spiritual achievements, and of most profound humility which the Gospel enjoins, frighten me by their very magnitude and in view of the weak and damaged state of my heart. So that I stand now between despair and hope. I don't know what will happen to me in the future.

The Skhimnik. With such an evident token of a special and miraculous mercy of God, and in view of your education, it would be unpardonable not only to give way to depression, but even to admit into your soul a shadow of doubt about God's protection and help. Do you know what the God-enlightened Chrysostom says about this? "No one should be depressed," he teaches, "and give the false impression that the precepts of the Gospel are impossible or impracticable. God who has predestined the salvation of man has, of course, not laid commandments upon him with the intention of making

him an offender because of their impracticability. No;
but so that by their holiness and the necessity of them
for a virtuous life they may be a blessing to us, as in this
life so in eternity." Of course the regular unswerving fulfilment of God's commandments is extraordinarily difficult for our fallen nature and, therefore, salvation is not
easily attained, but that same Word of God which lays
down the commandments offers also the means not only
for their ready fulfilment, but also comfort in the fulfilling of them. If this is hidden at first sight behind a veil
of mystery, then that, of course, is in order to make us
betake ourselves the more to humility, and to bring us
more easily into union with God by indicating direct re-
course to Him in prayer and petition for His fatherly
help. It is there that the secret of salvation lies, and not
in reliance upon one's own efforts.

The Pilgrim. How I should like, weak and feeble as I
am, to get to know that secret, so that I might to some
extent, at least, put my slothful life right, for the glory of
God and my own salvation.

The Skhimnik. The secret is known to you, dear
brother, from your book, *The Philokalia.* It lies in that
unceasing prayer of which you have made so resolute a
study and in which you have so zealously occupied
yourself and found comfort.

The Pilgrim. I fall at your feet, reverend Father. For
the love of God let me hear something for my good from
your lips about this saving mystery, and about holy
prayer, which I long to hear about more than anything
else, and about which I love reading to get strength and
comfort for my very sinful soul.

The Skhimnik. I cannot satisfy your wish with my
own thoughts on this exalted subject, because I have had
but very little experience of it myself. But I have some
very clearly written notes by a spiritual writer precisely
on this subject. If the rest of those who are talking with
us would like it, I will get it at once and with your permission I can read it to you all.

All. Do be so kind, reverend Father. Do not keep such saving knowledge from us.

THE SECRET OF SALVATION, REVEALED BY UNCEASING PRAYER

How is one saved? This godly question naturally arises in the mind of every Christian who realizes the injured and enfeebled nature of man, and what is left of its original urge towards truth and righteousness. Everyone who has even some degree of faith in immortality and recompense in the life to come is involuntarily faced by the thought, "How am I to be saved?" when he turns his eyes towards heaven. When he tries to find a solution of this problem, he enquires of the wise and learned. Then under their guidance he reads edifying books by spiritual writers on this subject, and sets himself unswervingly to follow out the truths and the rules he has heard and read. In all these instructions he finds constantly put before him as necessary conditions of salvation a devout life, and heroic struggles with himself which are to issue in decisive denial of self. This is to lead him on to the performance of good works, to the constant fulfilment of God's laws, and thus witness to the unshakableness and firmness of his faith. Further, they preach to him that all these conditions of salvation must necessarily be fulfilled with the deepest humility and in combination with one another. For as all good works depend one upon another, so they should support one another, complete and encourage one another, just as the rays of the sun only reveal their strength and kindle a flame when they are focused through a glass on to one point. Otherwise, *He that is unjust in the least is unjust also in much.*

In addition to this, to implant in him the strongest conviction of the necessity of this complex and unified virtue, he hears the highest praise bestowed upon the beauty of virtue, he listens to censure of the baseness and misery of vice. All this is imprinted upon his mind by truthful promises either of majestic rewards and happiness or of tormenting punishment and misery in the life to come. Such is the special character of preaching in modern times. Guided in this way, one who ardently wishes for salvation sets off in all joy to carry out what he has learned and to apply to experience all he has heard and read. But alas! even at the first step he finds it impossible to achieve his purpose. He foresees and even finds out by trial that his damaged and enfeebled nature will have the upper hand of the convictions of his mind, that his freewill is bound, that his propensities are perverted, that his spiritual strength is but weakness. He naturally goes on to the thought: Is there not to be found some kind of means which will enable him to fulfil that which the law of God requires of him, which Christian devotion demands, and which all those who have found salvation and holiness have carried out? As the result of this and in order to reconcile in himself the demands of reason and conscience with the inadequacy of his strength to fulfil them, he applies once more to the preachers of salvation with the question: How am I to be saved? How is this inability to carry out the conditions of salvation to be justified; and are those who have preached all this that he has learned themselves strong enough to carry it out unswervingly?

Ask God. Pray to God. Pray for His help.

"So would it not have been more fruitful," the enquirer concludes, "if I had, to begin with and always in every circumstance, made a study of prayer as the power to fulfil all that Christian devotion demands and by which salvation is attained?" And so he goes on to the study of prayer: he reads; he meditates; he studies the teaching of those who have written on that subject. Truly he finds in them many luminous thoughts, much deep knowledge and words of great power. One reasons beautifully about the necessity of prayer; another writes of its power, its beneficial effect—of prayer as a duty, or of the fact that it calls for zeal, attention, warmth of heart, purity of mind, reconciliation with one's enemies, humility, contrition, and the rest of the necessary conditions of prayer. But what is prayer in itself? How does one actually pray? A precise answer which can be understood by everybody to these questions, primary and most urgent as they are, is very rarely to be found, and so the ardent enquirer about prayer is again left before a veil

of mystery. As a result of his general reading
rooted in his memory an aspect of prayer which,
though devout, is only external, and he arrives at the
conclusion that prayer is going to church, crossing oneself, bowing, kneeling, reading psalms, *kanons* and
acathists.[29] Generally speaking, this is the view of prayer
taken by those who do not know the writings of the holy
Fathers about inward prayer and contemplative action.
At length, the seeker comes across the book called *Philokalia,* in which twenty-five holy Fathers set forth in an
understandable way the scientific knowledge of the truth
and of the essence of prayer of the heart. This begins to
draw aside the veil from before the secret of salvation
and of prayer. He sees that truly to pray means to direct
the thought and the memory, without relaxing, to the
recollection of God, to walk in His divine Presence, to
awaken oneself to His love by thinking about Him, and
to link the Name of God with one's breathing and the
beating of one's heart. He is guided in all this by the invocation with the lips of the most Holy Name of Jesus
Christ, or by saying the Jesus Prayer at all times and in
all places and during every occupation, unceasingly.
These luminous truths, by enlightening the mind of the
seeker and by opening up before him the way to the
study and achievement of prayer, help him to go on at
once to put these wise teachings into practice. Nevertheless, when he makes his attempts he is still not free from
difficulty until an experienced teacher shows him (from
the same book) the whole truth—that is to say, that it is
prayer which is incessant which is the only effective
means, alike for perfecting interior prayer and for the
saving of the soul. It is frequency of prayer which is the
basis, which holds together the whole system of saving
activity. As Simeon the New Theologian says, "He who
prays without ceasing unites all good in this one thing."

[29] *Acathist.* One of the many forms of the liturgical
hymnody of the Orthodox Church. Its characteristic is
praise. There are acathists of Our Lady and of the Saints.

The *Kanon* is another element which enters into the
structure of Eastern Orthodox Services. Further informa-
tion on this subject may be found in the writer's article on
Eastern Orthodox Services in *Liturgy and Worship*, p. 834.

So in order to set forth the truth of this revelation in all its fullness the teacher develops it in the following way:

For the salvation of the soul, first of all true faith is necessary. Holy Scripture says, *Without faith it is impossible to please God* (Heb. xi. 6). He who has not faith will be judged. But from the same Holy Scriptures one can see that man cannot himself bring to birth in him faith even as a grain of mustard seed; that faith does not come from us, since it is the gift of God; that faith is a spiritual gift. It is given by the Holy Spirit. That being so, what is to be done? How is one to reconcile man's need of faith with the impossibility of producing it from the human side? The way to do this is revealed in the same Holy Scriptures: *Ask, and it shall be given you.* The Apostles could not of themselves arouse the perfection of faith within them, but they prayed to Jesus Christ, *Lord, increase our faith.* There you have an example of obtaining faith. It shows that faith is attained by prayer. For the salvation of the soul, beside true faith, good works are also required, for *Faith, if it hath not works, is dead.* For man is judged by his works and not by faith alone. *If thou wilt enter into life, keep the commandements: Do not kill; do not commit adultery; do not steal; do not bear false witness; honour thy father and mother; love thy neighbour as thyself.* And all these commandments are required to be kept together. *For whosoever shall keep the whole law, and yet offend in one point, he is guilty of all* (Jas. ii. 10). So the Apostle James teaches. And the Apostle Paul, describing human weakness, says: *By the deeds of the law there shall no flesh be justified* (Rom. iii. 20). *For we know that the law is spiritual; but I am carnal, sold under sin. . . . For to will is present with me, but how to perform that which is good I find not. . . . But the evil which I would not, that I do. . . . With the mind I myself serve the law of God; but with the flesh the law of sin* (Rom. vii.). How are the required works of the law of God to be fulfilled when man is without strength, and has no power to keep the commandments? He has no possibility of doing this until he asks for it, until he prays about it. *Ye have not because ye ask not* (Jas. iv. 2) the Apostle says is the cause. And Jesus Christ Himself says: *Without Me ye can do nothing.* And on the subject of doing it with Him, He gives this teaching: *Abide in Me and I in you. He that abideth in Me and I in him, the same bringeth forth much fruit.* But to be in Him means continually to feel His presence, continually to pray in His Name. *If ye shall ask Me anything in My Name, that will I do.* Thus the possibility of doing good works is reached by prayer itself. An example of this is seen in the Apostle Paul himself: three times he prayed for victory over temptation, bowing the knee before God the Father, that He would give him strength in the inner man, and was at last bidden above all things to pray, and to pray continually about everything.

From what has been said above, it follows that the whole salvation of man depends upon prayer, and, therefore, it is primary and necessary, for by it faith is quickened and through it all good works are performed. In a word, with prayer everything goes forward successfully; without it, no act of Christian piety can be done. Thus, the condition that it should be offered unceasingly and always belongs exclusively to prayer. For the other Christian virtues, each of them has its own time. But in the case of prayer, uninterrupted, continuous action is commanded. *Pray without ceasing.* It is right and fitting to pray always, to pray everywhere. True prayer has its conditions. It should be offered with a pure mind and heart, with burning zeal, with close attention, with fear and reverence, and with the deepest humility. But what conscientious person would not admit that he is far from fulfilling those conditions, that he offers his prayer more from necessity, more by constraint upon himself than by inclination, enjoyment and love of it? About this, too, Holy Scripture says that it is not in the power of man to keep his mind steadfast, to cleanse it from unseemly thoughts, for the *thoughts of man are evil from his youth,* and that God alone gives us another heart and a new spirit, for *both to will and to do are of God.* The Apostle Paul himself says: *My spirit (that is, my voice) prayeth, but my understanding is unfruitful* (1 Cor. xiv. 14). *We know not what we should pray for as we ought* (Rom. viii. 26), the same writer asserts. From this it follows that we in ourselves are unable to offer true prayer. We cannot in our prayers display its essential properties.

Such being the powerlessness of every human being, what remains possible for the salvation of the soul from the side of human will and strength? Man cannot acquire faith without prayer; the same applies to good works. And, finally, even to pray purely is not within his power. What, then, is left for him to do? What scope remains for the exercise of his freedom and his strength, so that he may not perish but be saved?

Every action has its quality, and this quality God has reserved to His own will and gift. In order that the dependence of man upon God, the will of God, may be shown the more clearly, and that he may be plunged more deeply into humility, God has assigned to the will and strength of man only the *quantity* of prayer. He has commanded unceasing prayer, always to pray, at all times and in every place. By this the secret method of achieving true prayer, and at the same time faith, and the fulfilment of God's commandments, and salvation, are revealed. Thus, it is quantity which is assigned to man, as his share; frequency of prayer is his own, and within the province of his will. This is exactly what the Fathers of the Church teach. St. Macarius the Great says truly to pray is the gift of grace. Isikhi says that frequency of prayer becomes a habit and turns into second nature, and without frequent calling upon the Name of Jesus Christ it is impossible to cleanse the heart. The Venerable Callistus and Ignatius counsel frequent, continuous prayer in the Name of Jesus Christ before all ascetic exercises and good works, because frequency brings even the imperfect prayer to perfection. Blessed Diadokh asserts that if a man calls upon the Name of God as often as possible, then he will not fall into sin. What experience and wisdom there are here, and how near to the heart these practical instructions of the Fathers are. In their experience and simplicity they throw much light upon the means of bringing the soul to perfection. What a sharp contrast with the moral instructions of the theoretical reason! Reason argues thus: Do such and such good actions, arm yourself with

courage, use the strength of your will, persuade yourself
by considering the happy results of virtue—*e.g.*, cleanse
the mind and the heart from worldly dreams, fill their
place with instructive meditations; do good and you will
be respected and be at peace; live in the way that your
reason and conscience require. But alas! with all its
strength, all that does not attain its purpose without frequent prayer, without summoning the help of God.

Now let us go on to some further teaching of the
Fathers, and we shall see what they say, *e.g.*, about puri-
fying the soul. St. John of the Ladder writes: "When the
spirit is darkened by unclean thoughts, put the enemy to
flight by the Name of Jesus repeated frequently. A more
powerful and effective weapon than this you will not
find, in heaven or on earth." St. Gregory the Sinaite
teaches thus: "Know this, that no one can control his
mind by himself, and, therefore, at a time of unclean
thoughts call upon the Name of Jesus Christ often and
at frequent intervals, and the thoughts will quieten
down." How simple and easy a method! Yet it is tested
by experience. What a contrast with the counsel of the
theoretical reason, which presumptuously strives to attain to purity by its own efforts.

Noting these instructions based upon the experience
of the holy Fathers we pass on to the real conclusion:
that the principal, the only, and a very easy method of
reaching the goal of salvation and spiritual perfection is
the frequency and the uninterruptedness of prayer, however feeble it may be. Christian soul, if you do not find
within yourself the power to worship God in spirit and
in truth, if your heart still feels no warmth and sweet
satisfaction in mental and interior prayer, then bring to
the sacrifice of prayer what you can, what lies within the
scope of your will, what is within your power. Let the
humble instrument of your lips first of all grow familiar
with frequent persistent prayerful invocation. Let them
call upon the mighty Name of Jesus Christ often and
without interruption. This is not a great labour and is
within the power of everyone. This, too, is what the per-
cept of the Holy Apostle enjoins: *By Him, therefore, let
us offer the sacrifice of praise to God continually, that is,*

the fruit of our lips, giving thanks to His Name (Heb. xiii. 15).

Frequency of prayer certainly forms a habit and becomes second nature. It brings the mind and the heart into a proper state from time to time. Suppose a man continually fulfils this one commandment of God about ceaseless prayer, then in that one thing he would have fulfilled all; for if he uninterruptedly, at all times, and in all circumstances, offers the Prayer, calling in secret upon the most holy Name of Jesus (although at first he may do so without spiritual ardour and zeal and even forcing himself), then he will have no time for vain conversation, for judging his neighbours, for useless waste of time in sinful pleasures of the senses. Every evil thought of his would meet opposition to its growth. Every sinful act he contemplated would not come to fruition so readily as with an empty mind. Much talking and vain talking would be checked or entirely done away with, and every fault at once cleansed from the soul by the gracious power of so frequently calling upon the divine Name. The frequent exercise of prayer would often recall the soul from sinful action and summon it to what is the essential exercise of its skill, to union with God. Now do you see how important and necessary quantity is in prayer? Frequency in prayer is the one method of attaining pure and true prayer. It is the very best and most effective preparation for prayer, and the surest way of reaching the goal of prayer, and salvation.

To convince yourself finally about the necessity and fruitfulness of frequent prayer, note (1) that every impulse and every thought of prayer is the work of the Holy Spirit and the voice of your guardian angel; (2) that the Name of Jesus Christ invoked in prayer contains in itself self-existent and self-acting salutary power, and, therefore, (3) do not be disturbed by the imperfection or dryness of your prayer, and await with patience the fruit of frequently calling upon the divine Name. Do not listen to the inexperienced, thoughtless insinuation of the vain world that lukewarm invocation, even if it be importunate, is useless repetition. No; the power of the divine Name and the frequent calling upon it will reveal its fruit in its season. A certain spiritual writer has spoken very beautifully about this. "I know," he says, "that to many so-called spiritual and wise philosophers, who search everywhere for sham greatness and practices that are noble in the eyes of reason and pride, the simple, vocal, but frequent exercise of prayer appears of little significance, as a lowly occupation, even a mere trifle. But, unhappy ones, they deceive themselves, and they forget the teaching of Jesus Christ: *Except ye be converted and become as little children, ye shall not enter into the Kingdom of Heaven* (St. Matt. xviii. 3). They work out for themselves a sort of science of prayer, on the unstable foundations of the natural reason. Do we require much learning or thought or knowledge to say with a pure heart, "Jesus, Son of God, have mercy on me"? Does not our Divine Teacher Himself praise such frequent prayer? Have not wonderful answers been received and wonderful works done by this time brief but frequent prayer? Ah, Christian soul, pluck up your courage and do not silence the unbroken invocations of your prayer, although it may be that this cry of yours comes from a heart which is still at war with itself and half filled by the world. Never mind! Only go on with it and don't let it be silenced and don't be disturbed. It will itself purify itself by repetition. Never let your memory lose hold of this: *Greater is He that is in you than he that is in the world* (1 John iv. 4). *God is greater than our heart, and knoweth all things,* says the Apostle.

And so, after all these convincing arguments that frequent prayer, so powerful in all human weakness, is certainly attainable by man and lies fully within his own will, make up your mind to try, even if only for a single day at first. Maintain a watch over yourself and make the frequency of your prayer such that far more time is occupied in the twenty-four hours with the prayerful calling upon the Name of Jesus Christ than with other matters. And this triumph of prayer over worldly affairs will in time certainly show you that this day has not been lost, but has been secured for salvation; that in the scales of the divine judgment frequent prayer outweighs your weaknesses and evil-doing and blots out the sins of that day in the memorial book of conscience; that it sets your feet upon the ladder of righteousness and gives you hope of sanctification in the life to come.[30]

The Pilgrim. With all my heart I thank you, holy Father. With that reading of yours you have given pleasure to my sinful soul. For the love of God be so kind as to allow me to copy out for myself what you have read. I can do it in an hour or two. Everything you read was so beautiful and comforting and is so understandable and clear to my stupid mind, like *The Philokalia,* in which the holy Fathers treat the same subject. Here, for instance, John Karpathisky in the fourth part of *The Philokalia* also says that if you have not the strength for self-control and ascetic achievements, then know that God is willing to save you by prayer. But how beautifully and understandably all that is drawn out in your notebook. I thank God first of all, and then you, that I have been allowed to hear it.

The Professor. I also listened with great attention and pleasure to your reading, Reverend Father. All arguments, when they rest upon strict logic, are a delight to me. But at the same time it seems to me that they make the possibility of continual prayer in a high degree dependent on circumstances which are favourable to it and upon entirely quiet solitude. For I agree that frequent and ceaseless prayer is a powerful and unique means of obtaining the help of divine grace in all acts of devotion for the sanctifying of the soul, and that it is within the power of man. But this method can be used only when man avails himself of the possibility of solitude and quiet. In getting away from business and worries and distractions he can pray frequently or even continually. He then has to contend only with sloth or with the tedium of his own thoughts. But if he is bound by duties and by constant business, if he necessarily finds himself in a noisy company of people, and has an earnest desire to pray often, he cannot carry out this desire because of

[30] The original has a note here as follows: "From the author's MS. received by Father Ambrose of the Dobry Monastery."

the inevitable distractions. Consequently the one method of frequent prayer, since it is dependent upon favourable circumstances, cannot be used by everybody, nor belong to all.

The Skhimnik. It is no use drawing a conclusion of that kind. Not to mention the fact that the heart which has been taught interior prayer can always pray and call upon the Name of God unhindered during any occupation, whether of the body or of the mind, and in any noise (those who know this know it from experience, and those who do not know it must be taught by gradual training), one can confidently say that no outward distraction can interrupt prayer in one who wishes to pray, for the secret thought of man does not depend upon any link with external environment and is entirely free in itself. It can at all times be perceived and directed towards prayer; even the very tongue can secretly without outward sound express prayer in the presence of many people and during external occupations. Besides, our business is surely not so important and our conversation so interesting that it is impossible during them to find a way at times of frequently calling upon the Name of Jesus Christ, even if the mind has not yet been trained to continuous prayer. Although, of course, solitude and escape from distracting things does constitute the chief condition for attentive and continuous prayer, still we ought to feel ourselves to blame for the rarity of our prayer, because the amount and frequency is under the control of everybody, both the healthy and the sick. It does lie within the scope of his will. Instances which prove this are to be found in those who, although burdened by obligations, distracting duties, cares, worries and work, have not only always called upon the divine name of Jesus Christ, but even in this way learned and attained the ceaseless inward prayer of the heart. Thus the Patriarch Photius, who was called to the patriarchal dignity from among the ranks of the senators, while governing the vast diocese of Constantinople, persevered continually in the invocation of the Name of God, and thus attained even the self-acting prayer of the heart. Thus Callistus on the holy Mount Athos learned ceaseless prayer while carrying on his busy life as a cook. So the simple-hearted Lazarus, burdened with continual work for the brotherhood, uninterruptedly, in the midst of all his noisy occupations, repeated the Jesus Prayer and was at peace. And many others similarly have practised the continuous invocation of the Name of God.

If it were an impossible thing to pray midst distracting business or in the society of other people, then, of course, it would not have been bidden us. St. John Chrysostom, in his teaching about prayer, speaks as follows: "No one should give the answer that it is impossible for a man occupied with worldly cares, and who is unable to go to church, to pray always. Everywhere, wherever you may find yourself, you can set up an altar to God in your mind by means of prayer. And so it is fitting to pray at your trade, on a journey, standing at the counter or sitting at your handicraft. Everywhere and in every place it is possible to pray, and, indeed, if a man diligently turns his attention upon himself, then everywhere he will find convenient circumstances for prayer, if only he is convinced of the fact that prayer should constitute his chief occupation and come before every other duty. And in that case he would, of course, order his affairs with greater decision; in necessary conversation with other people he would maintain brevity, a tendency to silence, and a disinclination for useless words; he would not be unduly anxious about worrisome things. And in all these ways he would find more time for quiet prayer. In such an order of life all his actions, by the power of the invocation of the Name of God, would be signalized by success, and finally he would train himself to the uninterrupted prayerful invocation of the Name of Jesus Christ. He would come to know from experience that frequency of prayer, this sole means of salvation, is a possibility for the will of man, that it is possible to pray at all times, in all circumstances and in every place, and easily to rise from frequent vocal prayer to prayer of the mind and from that to prayer of the heart, which opens up the Kingdom of God within us."

The Professor. I agree that during mechanical occupations it is possible and even easy to pray frequently, even continuously; for mechanical bodily work does not require profound exercise of the mind or great consideration, and, therefore, while it is going on my mind can be immersed in continuous prayer and my lips follow in the same way. But if I have to be occupied with something exclusively intellectual, as, for instance, attentive reading, or thinking out some deep matter, or literary composition, how can I pray with my mind and my lips in such a case? And since prayer is above all things an action of the mind, how, at one and the same time, can I give one and the same mind different sorts of things to do?

The Skhimnik. The solution of your problem is not at all difficult, if we take into consideration that people who pray continuously are divided into three classes. First, the beginners; secondly, those who have made some progress; and, thirdly, the fully trained. Now, the beginners are frequently capable of experiencing at times an impulse of the mind and heart towards God and of repeating short prayers with the lips, even while engaged in mental work. Those who have made some progress and reached a certain stability of mind are able to occupy themselves with meditation or writing in the uninterrupted presence of God as the basis of prayer. The following example will illustrate this. Imagine that a severe and exacting monarch ordered you to compose a treatise on some abstruse subject in his presence, at the steps of his throne. Although you might be absolutely occupied by your work, the presence of the king who has power over you and who holds your life in his hands would still not allow you to forget for a single moment that you are thinking, considering and writing, not in solitude, but in a place which demands of you particular reverence, respect and decorum. This lively feeling of the nearness of the king very clearly expresses the possibility of being occupied in ceaseless inward prayer even during intellectual work. So far as the others are concerned, those who by long custom or by the mercy of

God have progressed from prayer of the mind and reached prayer of the heart, they do not break off their continuous prayer during profound mental exercises, nor even during sleep itself. As the All Wise has told us, *I sleep, but my heart waketh* (Cant. v. 2). Many, that is, who have achieved this mechanism of the heart acquire such an aptitude for calling upon the divine Name, that it will of itself arouse itself to prayer, incline the mind and the whole spirit to a flood of ceaseless prayer in whatever condition the one who prays finds himself, and however abstract and intellectual his occupation at the time.

The Priest. Allow me, reverend Father, to say what is in my mind. Let me have a turn and say a word or two. It was admirably put in the article you read that the one means of salvation and of reaching perfection is frequency of prayer, of whatever sort. Now, I do not very easily understand that, and it appears to me like this. What would be the use if I pray and invoke the Name of God continually with my tongue only and pay no attention to, and do not understand, what I am saying? That would be nothing but vain repetition. The result of it will only be that the tongue will go chattering on, and the mind, hindered in its meditations by this, will have its activity impaired. God does not ask for words, but for an attentive mind and a pure heart. Would it not be better to offer a prayer, be it only a short one, even rarely may be, or only at stated times, but with attention, with zeal and warmth of heart, and with due understanding? Otherwise, although you may say the prayer day and night, yet you have not got purity of mind, you are not performing a work of devotion, not achieving anything for your salvation. You are relying upon nothing but outward chatter, and you get tired and bored, and in the end the result is that your faith in prayer is completely chilled, and you throw over altogether this fruitless proceeding. Further, the uselessness of prayer with the lips only can be seen from what is revealed to us in Holy Scripture, as, for instance, *This people draweth nigh unto Me with their mouth and honoureth Me with their lips, but their heart is far from*

Me (St. Matt. xv. 8). *Not everyone that saith unto Me, Lord, Lord, shall enter into the Kingdom of Heaven* (St. Matt. vii. 21). *I had rather speak five words with my understanding . . . than ten thousand words in an unknown tongue* (1 Cor. xiv. 19). All this shows the fruitlessness of outward inattentive prayer with the mouth.

The Skhimnik. There might be something in your point of view if with the advice to pray with the mouth there were not added the need for it to be continuous, if prayer in the Name of Jesus Christ did not possess self-acting power and did not win for itself attention and zeal as a result of continuity in the exercise. But as the matter now in question is frequency, length of time, and uninterruptedness of prayer (although it may be carried on at first inattentively or with dryness), then, on account of this very fact, the conclusions that you mistakenly draw come to nothing. Let us look into the matter a little more closely. One spiritual writer, after arguing the very great value and fruitfulness of frequent prayer expressed in one form of words, says finally: "Many so called enlightened people regard this frequent offering of one and the same prayer as useless and even trifling, calling it mechanical and a thoughtless occupation of simple people. But unfortunately they do not know the secret which is revealed as a result of this mechanical exercise, they do not know how this frequent service of the lips imperceptibly becomes a genuine appeal of the heart, sinks down into the inward life, becomes a delight, becomes, as it were, natural to the soul, bringing it light and nourishment and leading it on to union with God." It seems to me that these censorious people are like those little children who were being taught the alphabet and how to read. When they got tired of it they cried out: "Would it not be a hundred times better to go fishing, like father, than to spend the whole day in ceaselessly repeating a, b, c, or scrawling on a sheet of paper with a pen?" The value of being able to read and the enlightenment which it brings, which they could have only as a result of this wearisome learning the letters by heart, was a hidden secret to them. In the same way the simple and frequent calling upon the Name of

God is a hidden secret to those people who are not persuaded of its results and its very great value. They, estimating the act of faith by the strength of their own inexperienced and short-sighted reason, forget, in so doing, that man has two natures, in direct influence one upon another, that man is made of body and soul. Why, for example, when you desire to purify your soul, do you first of all deal with your body, make it fast, deprive it of nourishment and stimulating food? It is, of course, in order that it may not hinder, or, to put it better, so that it may be the means of promoting purity of soul and enlightenment of mind, so that the continual feeling of bodily hunger may remind you of your resolution to seek for inward perfection and the things pleasing to God, which you so easily forget. And you find by experience that through the outward fast of your body you achieve the inward refining of your mind, the peace of your heart, an instrument for the taming of your passions and a reminder of spiritual effort. And thus, by means of outward and material things, you receive inward and spiritual profit and help. You must understand the same thing about frequent prayer with the lips, which by its long duration draws out the inward prayer of the heart, and promotes union of the mind with God. It is vain to imagine that the tongue, wearied by this frequency and barren lack of understanding, will be obliged to give up entirely this outward effort of prayer as useless. No; experience here shows us exactly the opposite. Those who have practised ceaseless prayer assure us that what happens is this: One who has made up his mind to call without ceasing upon the Name of Jesus Christ or, what is the same thing, to say the Jesus Prayer continuously, at first, of course, finds difficulty and has to struggle against sloth. But the longer and the harder he works at it, the more he grows familiar with the task imperceptibly, so that in the end the lips and the tongue acquire such capacity for moving themselves that even without any effort on his part they themselves act irresistibly and say the prayer voicelessly. At the same time the mechanism of the throat muscles is so trained that in praying he begins to feel that the saying of the prayer is a perpetual and essential property of himself, and even feels every time he stops as though something were missing in him. And so it results from this that his mind in its turn begins to yield, to listen to this involuntary action of the lips, and is aroused by it to attention which in the end becomes a source of delight to the heart, and true prayer.

There you see the true and beneficent effect of continuous or frequent vocal prayer, exactly the opposite of what people who have neither tried nor undertood it suppose. Concerning those passages in Holy Scripture which you brought forward in support of your objection, these are to be explained, if we make a proper examination of them. Hypocritical worship of God with the mouth, ostentation about it, or insincere praise in the cry, "Lord, Lord," Jesus Christ exposed for this reason, that the faith of the proud Pharisees was a matter of the mouth only, and in no degree did their conscience justify their faith, nor did they acknowledge it in their heart. It was to them that these things were said, and they do not refer to saying prayers, about which Jesus Christ gave direct, explicit and definite instructions. *Men ought to pray and not to faint.* Similarly, when the Apostle Paul says he prefers five words spoken with the understanding to a multitude of words without thought or in an unknown tongue in the Church, he is speaking about teaching in general, not about prayer in particular, on which subject he firmly says, *I will therefore that men pray every where* (1 Tim. ii. 8), and his is the general precept. *Pray without ceasing* (1 Thess. v. 17). Do you now see how fruitful frequent prayer is for all its simplicity, and what serious consideration the proper understanding of Holy Scripture requires?

The Pilgrim. Truly it is so, reverend Father. I have seen many who quite simply, without the light of any education whatever and not even knowing what attention is, offer the Prayer of Jesus with their mouths unceasingly. I have known them to reach a stage when their lips and tongue could not be restrained from saying the

prayer. It brought them such happiness and enlightenment, and changed them from weak and negligent people into *podvizhniki* and champions of virtue.[31]

The Skhimnik. Prayer brings a man to a new birth, as it
were. Its power is so great that nothing, no degree of
suffering will stand against it. If you like, by way of saying good-bye, brothers, I will read you a short but interesting article which I have with me.

All of them. We shall listen with the greatest pleasure.

The Skhimnik. ON THE POWER OF PRAYER
Prayer is so powerful, so mighty, that "pray, and do
what you like." Prayer will guide you to right and just
action. In order to please God nothing more is needed
than love. "Love, and do what you will," says the
blessed Augustine,[33] "for he who truly loves cannot wish
to do anything which is not pleasing to the one he
loves." Since prayer is the outpouring and the activity of
love, then one can truly say of it similarly, "Nothing
more is needed for salvation than continuous prayer."
"Pray, and do what you will," and you will reach the
goal of prayer. You will gain enlightenment by it.

[31] The original has a note here as follows: "In the nine-
ties of the last century there died at the Troitskaya Lavra[32]
a *starets,* a layman in his hundred and eighth year; he could
not read or write, but he said the Jesus Prayer even during
his sleep, and lived continually as the child of God, with a
heart that yearned for Him. His name was Gordi."

[32] *Troitskaya Lavra.* The famous monastery of the Holy
Trinity near Moscow, founded by St. Sergei in the fourteenth century. The part it played in Russian religious life
has been compared by Frere in some respects to the Clu-
niac movement (*Links in the Chain of Russian Church
History,* p. 36). The Troitskaya Lavra was intimately connected with Russian history, and was the focal point of the
national movement which drove out the Poles and placed
the first Romanov on the Russian throne in 1613.

[33] *St. Augustine.* The reference is to *Dilige, et quod vis
fac.* St. Augustine, Tract on the First Epistle of St. John,
Tract VII, Chapter X, paragraph 8, Edition Migne, III, p.
2033.

To draw out our understanding of this matter in more detail, let us take some examples:

(1) "Pray, and think what you will," your thoughts will be purified by prayer. Prayer will give you enlightenment of mind; it will remove and drive away all ill-judged thoughts. This is asserted by St. Gregory the Sinaite. If you wish to drive away thoughts and purify the mind his counsel is "drive them away by prayer." For nothing can control thoughts as prayer can. St. John of the Ladder also says about this: "Overcome the foes in your mind by the Name of Jesus. You will find no other weapon than this."

(2) "Pray, and do what you will." Your acts will be pleasing to God and useful and salutary to yourself. Frequent prayer, whatever it may be about, does not remain fruitless, because in it is the power of grace, *for whosoever shall call on the Name of the Lord shall be saved* (Acts ii. 21). For example: a man who had prayed without success and without devotion was granted through this prayer clearness of understanding and a call to repentence. A pleasure-loving girl prayed on her return home, and the prayer showed her the way to the virgin life and obedience to the teaching of Jesus Christ.

(3) "Pray, and do not labour much to conquer your passions by your own strength." Prayer will destroy them in you. *For greater is He that is in you than he that is in the world* (1 John iv. 4), says Holy Scripture. And St. John Karpathisky teaches that if you have not the gift of self-control, do not be cast down, but know that God requires of you diligence in prayer and the prayer will save you. The *starets* about whom we are told in the *Otechnik*[34] that, when he fell into sin, did not give way to depression, but betook himself to prayer and by it recovered his balance, is a case in point.

(4) "Pray, and fear nothing." Fear no misfortunes, fear no disasters. Prayer will protect you and ward them off. Remember St. Peter, who had little faith and was sinking; St. Paul, who prayed in prison; the monk who was delivered by prayer from the onset of temptation;

---

[34] *Otechnik.* Lives of the Fathers with extracts from their writings.

the girl who was saved from the evil purpose of a soldier as the result of prayer; and similar cases, which illustrate the power, the might, the universality of prayer in the Name of Jesus Christ.

(5) Pray somehow or other, only pray always and be disturbed by nothing. Be gay in spirit and peaceful. Prayer will arrange everything and teach you. Remember what the saints—John Chrysostom and Mark the Podvizhnik—say about the power of prayer. The first declares that prayer, even though it be offered by us who are full of sin, yet cleanses us at once. The latter says: "To pray somehow is within our power, but to pray purely is the gift of grace." So offer to God what it is within your power to offer. Bring to Him at first just quantity (which is within your power) and God will pour upon you strength in your weakness. "Prayer, dry and distracted may be, but continuous, will establish a habit and become second nature and turn itself into prayer which is pure, luminous, flaming and worthy."

(6) It is to be noted, finally, that if the time of your vigilance in prayer is prolonged, then naturally no time will be left not only for doing sinful actions but even for thinking of them.

Now, do you see what profound thoughts are focused in that wise saying: "Love, and do what you will"; "Pray, and do what you will"? How comforting and consoling is all this for the sinner overwhelmed by his weaknesses, groaning under the burder of his warring passions.

Prayer—there you have the whole of what is given to us as the universal means of salvation and of growth of the soul into perfection. Just that. But when prayer is named, a condition is added. *Pray without ceasing* is the command of God's Word. Consequently prayer shows its most effective power and fruit when it is offered often, ceaselessly; for frequency of prayer undoubtedly belongs to our will, just as purity, zeal and perfection in prayer are the gifts of grace.

And so we will pray as often as we can; we will consecrate our whole life to prayer, even if it be subject to distractions to begin with. Frequent practice of it will teach us attentiveness. Quantity will certainly lead on to quality. "If you want to learn to do anything whatever well you must do it as often as possible," said an experienced spiritual writer.

The Professor. Truly prayer is a great matter, and ardent frequency of it is the key to open the treasury of its grace. But how often I find a conflict in myself between ardour and sloth. How glad I should be to find the way to gain the victory and to convince myself and arouse myself to continuous application to prayer.

The Skhimnik. Many spiritual writers offer a number of ways based upon sound reasoning for stimulating diligence in prayer. For example, (1) they advise you to steep your mind in thoughts of the necessity, the excellence, and the fruitfulness of prayer for saving the soul; (2) make yourself firmly convinced that God absolutely requires prayer of us and that His Word everywhere commands it; (3) always remember that if you are slothful and careless about prayer you can make no progress in acts of devotion nor in attaining peace and salvation, and, therefore, will inevitably suffer both punishment on earth and torment in the life to come; (4) enhearten your resolution by the example of the saints who all attained holiness and salvation by the way of continuous prayer.

Although all these methods have their value and arise from genuine understanding, yet the pleasure-loving soul which is sick with listlessness, even when it has accepted and used them, rarely sees the fruit of them, for this reason: that these medicines are bitter to its impaired sense of taste and too weak for its deeply injured nature. For what Christian is there who does not know that he ought to pray aften and diligently, that God requires it of him, that we are punished for sloth in prayer, that all the saints have ardently and constantly prayed? Nevertheless, how rarely does all this knowledge show good results. Every observer of himself sees that he justifies but little, and but rarely, these promptings of reason and conscience, and through infrequent remembrance of them lives all the while in the same bad and slothful way. And so, in their experience and godly

wisdom, the holy Fathers, knowing the weakness of will
and the exaggerated love of pleasure in the heart of
man, take a special line about it, and in this respect put
jam with the powder and smear the edge of the medi-
cine-cup with honey. They show the easiest and most
effective means of doing away with sloth and indifference in prayer, in the hope, with God's help, of attaining by prayer to perfection and the sweet expectation of
love for God.

They advise you to meditate as often as possible
about the state of your soul and to read attentively what
the Fathers have written on the subject. They give en-
couraging assurance that these enjoyable inward feelings my be readily and easily attained in prayer, and say
how much they are to be desired. Heartfelt delight, a
flood of inward warmth and light, ineffable enthusiasm,
joy, lightness of heart, profound peace and the very essence of blessedness and happy content, are all results of
prayer in the heart. By steeping itself in such reflections
as these, the weak cold soul is kindled and strengthened,
it is encouraged by ardour for prayer, and is, as it were,
enticed to put the practice of prayer to the test. As St.
Isaac the Syrian says: "Joy is an enticement to the soul,
joy which is the outcome of hope blossoming in the
heart, and meditation upon its hope is the well-being of
the heart."

The same writer continues: "At the outset of this activity and right to the end there is presupposed some
sort of method and hope for its completion, and this
both arouses the mind to lay a foundation for the task
and from the vision of its goal the mind borrows consolation during the labour of reaching it." In the same way
St. Isikhi, after describing the hindrance that sloth is to
prayer and clearing away misconceptions about the renewal of ardour for it, finally says outright: "If we are
not ready to desire the silence of the heart for any other
reason, then let it be for the delightful feeling of it in the
soul and for the gladness that it brings." It follows
from this that this Father gives the enjoyable feeling of
gladness as an incitement to assiduity in prayer, and in
the same way Macarius the Great teaches that our spiritual efforts (prayer) should be carried out with the

purpose and in the hope of producing fruit—that is, enjoyment in our hearts. Clear instances of the potency of this method are to be seen in very many passages of *The Philokalia*, which contains detailed descriptions of the delights of prayer. One who is struggling with the infirmity of sloth or dryness in prayer ought to read them over as often as possible, considering himself, however, unworthy of these enjoyments and ever reproaching himself for negligence in prayer.

The Priest. Will not such meditation lead the inexperienced person to spiritual voluptuousness, as the theologians call that tendency of the soul which is greedy of excessive consolation and sweetness of grace, and is not content to fulfil the work of devotion from a sense of obligation and duty without dreaming about reward?

The Professor. I think that the theologians in this case are warning men against excess or greed of spiritual happiness, and are not entirely rejecting enjoyment and consolation in virtue. For if the desire for reward is not perfection, nevertheless God has not forbidden man to think about rewards and consolation, and even Himself uses the idea of reward to incite men to fulfil His commandments and to attain perfection. *Honour thy father and thy mother*. There is the command and you see the reward follows as a spur to its fulfilment, *and it shall be well with thee. If thou wilt be perfect, go, sell all that thou hast and come and follow Me*. There is the demand for perfection, and immediately upon it comes the reward as an inducement to attain perfection, *and thou shalt have treasure in heaven. Blessed are ye when men shall hate you, and when they shall separate you from their company, and shall reproach you, and cast out your name as evil, for the Son of Man's sake* (St. Luke vi. 22). There is a great demand for a spiritual achievement which needs unusual strength of soul and unshakable patience. And so for that there is a great reward and consolation, which are able to arouse and maintain this unusual strength of soul—*For your reward is great in heaven*. For this reason I think that a certain desire for enjoyment in prayer of the heart is necessary and probably constitutes the means of attaining both diligence and success in it. And so all this undoubtedly supports the practical teaching on this subject which we have just heard from the Father Skhimnik.

The Skhimnik. One of the great theologians—that is to say, St. Macarius of Egypt—speaks in the clearest possible way about this matter. He says: "As when you are planting a vine you bestow your thought and labour with the purpose of gathering the vintage, and if you do not, all your labour will be useless, so also in prayer, if you do not look for spiritual fruit—that is, love, peace, joy and the rest—your labour will be useless. And, therefore, we ought to fulfil our spiritual duties (prayer) with the purpose and hope of gathering fruit—that is to say, comfort and enjoyment in our hearts." Do you see how clearly the holy Father answers this question about the need for enjoyment in prayer? And, as a matter of fact, there has just come into my mind a point of view which I read not long ago of a writer on spiritual things, to this effect: that the naturalness of prayer to man is the chief cause of his inclination towards it. So the examination of this naturalness, in my opinion, may also serve as a potent means of arousing diligence in prayer, the means which the Professor is so eagerly looking for.

Let me now sum up shortly some points I drew attention to in that notebook. For instance, the writer says that reason and nature lead man to the knowledge of God. The first investigates the fact that there cannot be action without cause and ascending the ladder of tangible things from the lower to the higher, at last reaches the first Cause, God. The second displays at every step its marvellous wisdom, harmony, order, gradation, gives the basic material for the ladder which leads from finite causes to the infinite. Thus, the natural man arrives naturally at the knowledge of God. And, therefore, there is not, and never has been, any people, any barbarous tribe, without some knowledge of God. As a result of this knowledge the most savage islander, without any impulse from outside, as it were, involuntarily raises his gaze to heaven, falls on his knees, breathes out a sigh which he does not understand, necessary as it is, and has a direct feeling that there is something which draws him upwards, something urging him towards the unknown. From this foundation all natural religions arise. And in this connection it is very remarkable that universally the essence or the soul of every religion consists in secret prayer, which shows itself in some form of movement of the spirit and what is clearly an oblation, though more or less distorted by the darkness of the coarse and wild understanding of heathen people. The more surprising this fact is in the eyes of reason, the greater is the demand upon us to discover the hidden cause of this wonderful thing which finds expression in a natural movement towards prayer. The psychological answer to this is not difficult to find. The root, the head and the strength of all passions and actions in man is his innate love of self. The deep-rooted and universal idea of self-preservation clearly confirms this. Every human wish, every undertaking, every action has as its purpose the satisfaction of self-love, the seeking of the man's own happiness. The satisfaction of this demand accompanies the natural man all through his life. But the human spirit is not satisfied with anything that belongs to the senses, and the innate love of self never abates its urgency. And so desires develop more and more, the endeavour to attain happiness grows stronger, fills the imagination and incites the feelings to this same end. The flood of this inward feeling and desire as it develops is the natural arousing to prayer. It is a requirement of self-love which attains its purpose with difficulty. The less the natural man succeeds in attaining happiness and the more he has it in view, the more his longing grows and the more he finds an outlet for it in prayer. He betakes himself in petition for what he desires to the unknown Cause of all being. So it is that innate self-love, the principal element in life, is a deep-seated stimulus to prayer in the natural man. The all-wise Creator of all things has imbued the nature of man with a capacity for self-love precisely as an "enticement," to use the expression of the Fathers, which will draw the fallen being of man upwards into touch with celestial things. Oh! if man had not spoilt this capacity, if only he had kept it in its excellence, in touch with his spiritual nature! Then he would have had a powerful incentive and an effective means of bringing him along the road to moral perfection. But, alas! how often he makes of this noble capacity a base passion of self-love when he turns it into an instrument of his animal nature.

The Starets. I thank you from my heart, all my dear visitors. Your salutary conversation has been a great consolation to me and taught me, in my inexperience, many profitable things. May God give you His grace in return for your edifying love.
[*They all separate.*]

7

THE PILGRIM. My devout friend the Professor and I could not resist our desire to start on our journey, and before doing so to look in and say a last good-bye to you and ask for your prayers.

The Professor. Yes, our intimacy with you has meant a great deal to us, and so have the salutary conversations on spiritual things which we have enjoyed at your house in company with your friends. We shall keep the memory of all this in our hearts as a pledge of fellowship and Christian love in that distant land to which we are hastening.

The Starets. Thank you for remembering me. And, by the way, how opportune your arrival is. There are two travellers stopping with me, a Moldavian monk and a hermit who has lived in silence for twenty-five years in a forest. They want to see you. I will call them at once. Here they are.

The Pilgrim. Ah, how blessed a life of solitude is! And how suitable for bringing the soul into unbroken union with God! The silent forest is like a Garden of Eden in which the delightful tree of life grows in the prayerful heart of the recluse. If I had something to live on, nothing, I think, would keep me from the life of a hermit!

The Professor. Everything seems particularly desirable to us from a distance. But we all find out by experience that every place, though it may have its advantages, has its drawbacks too. Of course, if one is melancholy by temperament, and inclined to silence, then a solitary life is a comfort. But what a lot of dangers lie along that road. The history of the ascetic life provides many instances to show that numbers of recluses and hermits, having entirely deprived themselves of human society, have fallen into self-deception and profound seductions.

The Hermit. I am surprised at how often one hears it said in Russia, not only in religious houses, but even among God-fearing lay-folk, that many who desire the hermit life, or exercise in the practice of interior prayer, are held back from following up this inclination by the fear that seductions will ruin them. Insisting on this, they bring forward instances of the conclusion their minds have arrived at as a reason alike for avoiding the interior life themselves and for keeping other people from it also. To my mind this arises from two causes: either from failure to understand the task and lack of spiritual enlightenment, or from their own indifference to contemplative achievement and jealousy lest others who are at a low level in comparison with themselves should out-distance them in this higher knowledge. It is a great pity that those who hold this conviction do not investigate the teaching of the holy Fathers on the matter, for they very decidedly teach that one ought neither to fear nor to doubt when one calls upon God. If certain of them have indeed fallen into self-deception and fanaticism, that was the result of pride, of not having a director, and of taking appearances and imagination for reality. Should such a time of testing occur, they continue, it would lead to experience and a crown of glory, for the help of God comes swiftly to protect when such a thing is permitted. Be courageous. *I am with you, fear not,* says Jesus Christ. And it follows from this that to feel fear and alarm at the interior life on the pretext of the risk of self-deception is a vain thing. For humble consciousness of one's sins, openness of soul with one's director, and "formlessness" in prayer are a strong and safe defence against those tempting illusions of which many feel so great a fear and, therefore, do not embark upon activity of the mind. Incidentally these very people find themselves exposed to temptation, as the wise words of Philotheus the Sinaite tell us. He says: "There are many monks who do not understand the illusion of their own minds, which they suffer at the hands of demons—that is to say, they give themselves diligently to only one form of activity, 'outward good works'; whereas of the mind—that is, of inward contemplation—they have little care, since they are unenlightened and ignorant about this." "Even if they hear of others that grace works inwardly within them, through jealousy they regard it as self-deception," St. Gregory the Sinaite declares.

The Professor. Allow me to ask you a question. Of course the consciousness of one's sins is proper for everyone who pays any attention to himself. But how does one proceed when no director is available to guide one in the way of the interior life from his own experience, and when one has opened one's heart to him, to impart to one correct and trustworthy knowledge about the spiritual life? In that case, no doubt, it would be better not to attempt contemplation rather than try it on one's own without a guide? Further: for my part, I don't readily understand how, if one puts oneself in the presence of God, it is possible to observe complete "formlessness." It is not natural, for our soul or our mind can present nothing to the imagination without form, in absolute formlessness. And why, indeed, when the mind is steeped in God, should we not present to the imagination Jesus Christ, or the Holy Trinity, and so on?

The Hermit. The guidance of a director or *starets* who is experienced and knowledgeable in spiritual things, to whom one can open one's heart every day without hindrance, with confidence and advantage, and tell one's thoughts and what one has met with on the path of interior schooling, is the chief condition for the practice of prayer of the heart by one who has entered upon the life of silence. Yet, in cases where it is impossible to find such a one, the same holy Fathers who prescribe this make an exception. Nicephorus the Monk gives clear instructions about it, thus: "During the practice of inward activity of the heart, a genuine and well-

informed director is required. If such a one is not at
hand, then you must diligently search for one. If you do
not find him, then, calling contritely upon God for help,
draw instruction and guidance from the teaching of the
holy Fathers and verify it from the Word of God set
forth in the Holy Scriptures." Here one must also take
into consideration the fact that the seeker of goodwill
and zeal can obtain something useful in the way of instruction from ordinary people also. For the holy Fathers assure us likewise, that if with faith and right intention one questions even a Saracen, he can speak words
of value to us. If, on the other hand, one asks for instruction from a Prophet, without faith and a righteous
purpose, then even he will not satisfy us. We see an instance of this in the case of Macarius the Great of
Egypt, to whom on one occasion a simple villager gave
an explanation which put an end to the distress which he
was experiencing.

As regards "formlessness"—that is, not using the imagination and not accepting any sort of vision during
contemplation, whether of light, or of an angel, or of
Christ, or any saint, and turning aside from all dreaming
—this, of course, is enjoined by experienced holy Fathers for this reason: that the power of the imagination
may easily incarnate or, so to speak, give life to the rep-
resentations of the mind, and thus the inexperienced
might readily be attracted by these figments, take them
as visions of grace, and fall into self-deception, in spite
of the fact that Holy Scripture says that Satan himself
may assume the form of an angel of light. And that the
mind can naturally and easily be in a state of "formlessness" and keep so, even while recollecting the presence
of God, can be seen from the fact that the power of the
imagination can perceptibly present a thing in "formlessness" and maintain its hold upon such a presenta-
tion. Thus, for example, the representation of our souls,
of the air, warmth, or cold. When you are cold you can
have a lively idea of warmth in your mind, though
warmth has no shape, is not an object of sight, and is
not measured by the physical feeling of one who finds
himself in the cold. In the same way also the presence of

the spiritual and incomprehensible Being of God may be present to the mind and recognized in the heart in absolute "formlessness."

The Pilgrim. During my wanderings I have come across people, devout people, who were seeking salvation, who have told me that they were afraid to have anything to do with the interior life, and denounced it as a mere illusion. To several of them I read out of *The Philokalia* the teaching of St. Gregory the Sinaite with some profit. He says that "the action of the heart cannot be an illusion (as that of the mind can), for if the Enemy desired to turn the warmth of the heart into his own uncontrolled fire, or to change the gladness of the heart into the dull pleasures of the senses, still time, experience, and the feeling itself would expose his craftiness and cunning, even for those who are not very learned." I have also met other people who, most unhappily, after knowing the way of silence and prayer of the heart, have on meeting some obstacle or sinful weakness given way to depression, and given up the inward activity of the heart which they had known.

The Professor. Yes, and that is very natural. I have myself experienced the same thing at times, on occasions when I have lapsed from the interior frame of mind or done something wrong. For since inward prayer of the heart is a holy thing, and union with God, is it not unseemly and a thing not to be dared to bring a holy thing into a sinful heart, without having first purified it by silent contrite penitence and a proper preparation for communion with God? It is better to be dumb before God than to offer Him thoughtless words out of a heart which is in darkness and distraction.

The Monk. It is a great pity that you think like that. That is despondency, which is the worst of all sins and constitutes the principal weapon of the world of darkness against us. The teaching of our experienced holy Fathers about this is quite different. Nicetas Stethatus says that if you have fallen and sunk down even into the depths of hellish evil, even then you are not to despair, but to turn quickly to God, and He will speedily raise up your fallen heart and give you more strength than you had before. So after every fall and sinful wounding of the heart the thing to do is immediately to place it in the Presence of God for healing and cleansing, just as things that have become infected, if they are exposed for some time to the power of the sun's rays, lose the sharpness and strength of their infection. Many spiritual writers speak positively about this inner conflict with the enemies of salvation, our passions. If you receive wounds a thousand times, still you should by no means give up the life-giving action—that is to say, calling upon Jesus Christ who is present in our hearts. Our actions not only ought not to turn us away from walking in the Presence of God and from inward prayer, and so produce disquiet, depression and sadness in us, but rather further our swift turning to God. The infant who is led by its mother when it begins to walk turns quickly to her and holds on to her firmly when it stumbles.

The Hermit. I look at it in this way, that the spirit of despondency, and agitating and doubting thoughts, are aroused most easily by distraction of the mind and failure to guard the silent resort of one's inner self. The ancient Fathers in their divine wisdom won the victory over despondency and received inward light and strength through hope in God, through peaceful silence and solitude, and they have given us wise and useful counsel: "sit silently in your cell and it will teach you everything."

The Professor. I have such confidence in you that I listen very gladly to your critical analysis of my thoughts about the silence which you praise so highly, and the benefits of the solitary life which hermits so love to lead. Well, this is what I think: Since all people, by the law of nature ordained by the Creator, are placed in necessary dependence upon one another and, therefore, are bound to help one another in life, to labour for one another and to be of service to one another, this sociability makes for the well-being of the human race and shows love for one's neighbour. But the silent hermit who has withdrawn from human society, in what way can he, in his inactivity, be of service to his neighbour and what contribution can he make to the well-being of human society? He completely destroys in himself that law of the Creator which concerns union in love of one's kind and beneficent influence upon the brotherhood.

The Hermit. Since this view of yours about silence is incorrect, the conclusion you draw from it will not hold good. Let us consider it in detail. (1) The man who lives in silent solitude is not only not living in a state of inactivity and idleness; he is in the highest degree active, even more than the one who takes part in the life of society. He untiringly acts according to his highest rational nature; he is on guard; he ponders; he keeps his eye upon the state and progress of his moral existence. This is the true purpose of silence. And in the measure that this ministers to his own improvement, it benefits others for whom undistracted submergence within themselves for the development of the moral life is impossible. For he who watches in silence, by communicating his inward experiences either by word (in exceptional cases) or by committing them to writing, promotes the spiritual advantage and the salvation of his brethren. And he does more, and that of a higher kind, than the private benefactor, because the private, emotional charities of people in the world are always limited by the small number of benefits conferred, whereas he who confers benefits by morally attaining to convincing and tested means of perfecting the spiritual life becomes a benefactor of whole peoples. His experience and teaching pass on from generation to generation, as we see ourselves and of which we avail ourselves from ancient times to this day. And this in no sense differs from Christian love; it even surpasses it in its results. (2) The beneficent and most useful influence of the man who observes silence upon his neighbours is not only shown in the communication of his instructive observations upon the interior life, but also the very example of his separated life benefits the attentive layman by leading him to self-knowledge and arousing in him the feeling of reverence. The man who lives in the world, hearing of the devout recluse, or going past the door of his hermitage, feels an impulse to the devout life, has recalled to his mind what man can be upon earth, that it is possible for man to get back to that primitive contemplative state in which he issued from the hands of his Creator. The silent recluse teaches by his very silence, and by his very life he benefits, edifies and persuades to the search for God. (3) This benefit springs from genuine silence which is illuminated and sanctified by the light of grace. But if the silent one did not have these gifts of grace which make him a light to the world, even if he should have embarked upon the way of silence with the purpose of hiding himself from the society of his kind as the result of sloth and indifference, even then he would confer a great benefit upon the community in which he lives, just as the gardner cuts off dry and barren branches and clears away the weeds so that the growth of the best and most useful may be unimpeded. And this is a great deal. It is of general benefit that the silent one by his seclusion removes the temptations which would inevitably arise from his unedifying life among people and be injurious to the morals of his neighbours.

On the subject of the importance of silence, St. Isaac the Syrian exclaims as follows: "When on one side we place all the actions of this life and on the other silence, we find that it weighs down the scales. Do not place those who perform signs and wonders in the world on a level with those who keep silence with knowledge. Love the inactivity of silence more than the satiety of greedy ones in the world and the turning of many people to God. It is better for you to cut yourself free from the bonds of sin than to liberate slaves from their servitude." Even the most elementary sages have recognized the value of silence. The philosophical school of the Neoplatonists, which embraced many adherents under the guidance of the philosopher Plotinus, developed to a high degree the inner contemplative life which is attained most especially in silence. One spiritual writer said that if the State were developed to the highest degree of education and morals, yet even then it would still be necessary to provide people for contemplation, in addition to the general activities of citizens, in order to preserve the spirit of truth, and having received it from all the centuries that are past, to keep it for the generations to come and hand it on to posterity. Such people, in the Church, are hermits, recluses and anchorites.

The Pilgrim. I think that no one has so truly valued the excellences of silence as St. John of the Ladder. "Silence," he says, "is the mother of prayer, a return from the captivity of sin, unconscious success in virtue, a continuous ascension to heaven." Yes, and Jesus Christ Himself, in order to show us the advantage and necessity of silent seclusion, often left His public preaching and went into silent places for prayer and quietude. The silent contemplates are like pillars supporting the devotion of the Church by their secret continuous prayer. Even in the distant past one sees that many devout layfolk, and even kings and their courtiers, went to visit hermits and men who kept silence in order to ask them to pray for their strengthening and salvation. Thus the silent recluse, too, can serve his neighbour and act to the advantage and the happiness of society by his secluded prayer.

The Professor. Now, there again, that is a thought which I do not very easily understand. It is a general custom among all of us Christians to ask for each other's prayers, to want another to pray for me, and to have special confidence in a member of the Church. Is not this simply a demand of self-love? Is it not that we have only caught the habit of saying what we have heard others say, as a sort of fancy of the mind without any serious consideration? Does God require human intercession, since He foresees everything and acts according to His all-blessed Providence and not according to our desire, knowing and settling everything before our petition is made, as the Holy Gospel says? Can the prayer of many people really be any stronger to overcome His decisions than the prayer of one person? In that case God would be a respecter of persons. Can the prayer of another person really save me when everybody is commended or put to shame on the ground of his own actions? And, therefore, the request for the prayers of an-

other person is to my mind merely a pious expression of
spiritual courtesy, which shows signs of humility and a
desire to please by preferring one another, and that is
all.

The Monk. If one take only outward considerations
into account, and with an elementary philosophy, it
might be put in that way. But the spiritual reason
blessed by the light of religion and trained by the experiences of the interior life goes a good deal deeper, contemplates more clearly, and in a mystery reveals something entirely different from what you have put forward.
So that we may understand this more quickly and clearly, let us take an example and then verify the truth of it
from the Word of God. Let us say that a pupil came to a
certain teacher for instruction. His feeble capacities and,
what is more, his idleness and lack of concentration prevented him from attaining any success in his studies and
they put him in the category of the idle and unsuccess-
ful. Feeling sad at this he did not know what to do, nor
how to contend with his deficiencies. Then he met another pupil, a class-mate of his, who was more able than
he, more diligent and successful, and he explained his
trouble to him. The other took an interest in him, and
invited him to work with him. "Let us work together,"
he said, "and we shall be keener, more cheerful and,
therefore, more successful." And so they began to study
together, each sharing with the other what he understood. The subject of their study was the same. And
what followed after several days? The indifferent one
became diligent; he came to like his work, his careless-
ness was changed to ardour and intelligence, which had
a beneficial effect upon his character and morals also.
And the intelligent one in his turn became more able
and industrious. In the effect they had upon one another they arrived at a common advantage. And this is very
natural, for man is born in the society of people; he develops his rational understanding through people, habits
of life, training, emotions, the action of the will—in a
word, everything he receives from the example of his
kind. And, therefore, as the life of men consists in the
closest relations and the strongest influences of one upon

another, he who lives among a certain sort of people becomes accustomed to that kind of habit, behaviour and morals. Consequently the cool become enthusiastic, the stupid become sharp, the idle are aroused to activity by a lively interest in their fellow-men. Spirit can give itself to spirit and act beneficially upon another and attract another to prayer, to attention. It can encourage him in despondency, turn him from vice, and arouse him to holy action. And so by helping each other they can become more devout, more energetic spiritually, more reverent. There you have the secret of prayer for others, which explains the devout custom on the part of Christian people of praying for one another and asking for the prayers of the brethren.

And from this one can see that it is not that God is pleased, as the great ones of this world are, by a great many petitions and intercessions, but that the very spirit and power of prayer cleanses and arouses the soul for whom the prayer is offered and presents it ready for union with God. If mutual prayer by those who are living upon earth is so beneficial, then in the same way we may infer that prayer for the departed also is mutually beneficial because of the very close link that exists between the heavenly world and this. In this way souls of the Church Militant can be drawn into union with souls of the Church Triumphant, or, what is the same thing, the living with the dead.

All that I have said is psychological reasoning, but if we open Holy Scripture we can verify the truth of it. (1) Jesus Christ says to the Apostle Peter, *I have prayed for thee, that thy faith fail not.* There you see that the power of Christ's prayer strengthens the spirit of St. Peter and encourages him when his faith is tested. (2) When the Apostle Peter was kept in prison, *prayer was made without ceasing of the church unto God for him.* Here we have revealed the help which brotherly prayer gives in the troubled circumstances of life. (3) But the clearest precept about prayer for others is put by the holy Apostle James in this way, *Confess your sins one to another, and pray for one another. . . . The effectual fervent prayer of a righteous man availeth much.* Here is definite confirmation of the psychological argument above. And what are we to say of the example of the holy Apostle Paul, which is given to us as the pattern of prayer for one another? One writer observes that this example of the holy Apostle Paul should teach us how necessary prayer for one another is, when so holy and strong a *podvizhnik* acknowledges his own need of this spiritual help. In the Epistle to the Hebrews he words his request in this way: *Pray for us: for we trust we have a good conscience, in all things willing to live honestly* (Heb. xiii. 18). When we take note of this, how unreasonable it seems to rely upon our own prayers and successes only, when a man so holy, so full of grace, in his humility asks for the prayers of his neighbours (the Hebrews) to be joined to his own. Therefore, in humility, simplicity and unity of love we should not reject or disdain the help of the prayers of even the feeblest of believers when the clear-sighted spirit of the Apostle Paul felt no hesitation about it. He asks for the prayers of all in general, knowing that the power of God is made perfect in weakness. Consequently it can at times be made perfect in those who seem able to pray but feebly. Feeling the force of this example, we notice further that prayer one for another strengthens that unity in Christian love which is commanded by God, witnesses to humility in the spirit of him who makes the request, and, so to speak, attracts the spirit of him who prays. Mutual intercession is stimulated in this way.

The Professor. Your analysis and your proofs are admirable and exact, but it would be interesting to hear from you the actual method and form of prayer for others. For I think that if the fruitfulness and attractive power of prayer depend upon a living interest in our neighbours, and conspicuously upon the constant influence of the spirit of him who prays upon the spirit of him who asked for prayer, such a state of soul might draw one away from the uninterrupted sense of the invisible Presence of God and the outpouring of one's soul before God in one's own needs. And if one brings one's neighbour to mind just once or twice in the day, with sympathy for him, asking the help of God for him, would that not be enough for the attracting and

strengthening of his soul? To put it briefly,
to know exactly how to pray for others.

The Monk. Prayer which is offered to C̶ ... anything whatever ought not, and cannot, take us away
from the sense of the Presence of God, for if it is an offering made to God, then, of course, it must be in His
Presence. So far as the method of praying for others is
concerned, it must be noted that the power of this sort
of prayer consists in true Christian sympathy with one's
neighbour, and it has an influence upon his soul according to the extent of that sympathy. Therefore, when one
happens to remember him (one's neighbour), or at the
time appointed for doing so, it is well to bring a mental
view of him into the Presence of God, and to offer prayer in the following form: "Most merciful God, Thy will
be done, which will have all men to be saved and to
come unto the knowledge of the truth, save and help
Thy servant N. Take this desire of mine as a cry of love
which Thou hast commanded." Commonly you will repeat those words when your soul feels moved to do so,
or you might tell your beads with this prayer. I have
found from experience how beneficially such a prayer
acts upon him for whom it is offered.

The Professor. Your views and arguments and the
edifying conversation and illuminating thoughts which
spring from them are such that I shall feel bound to
keep them in my memory, and to give you all the reverence and thanks of my grateful heart.

The Pilgrim and the Professor. The time has come for
us to go. Most heartily we ask for your prayers upon our
journey and upon our companionship.

*The Starets. The God of peace that brought again
from the dead our Lord Jesus, that great shepherd of the
sheep, through the blood of the everlasting covenant,
make you perfect in every good work to do His will,
working in you that which is well pleasing in His sight,
through Jesus Christ; to whom be glory for ever and
ever. Amen* (Heb. xiii, 20, 21).

BIOGRAPHICAL NOTES

ANTHONY THE GREAT was born about A.D. 250 in Egypt. As a young man he adopted the solitary life of the ascetic and was perhaps the first to withdraw into the desert to live a hermit life. His influence spread widely and he kept in touch with his friend St. Athanasius the Great who wrote his *Life*.

BASIL THE GREAT. Bishop of Cæsarea in Cappadocia in the fourth century. A great writer and preacher, he was a reformer also in the spheres of the Liturgy and the monastic life. The "Liturgy of St. Basil" is used by the Orthodox on Sundays in Lent and a few other days. Orthodox monks and nuns follow the Rule of St. Basil.

BLESSED DIADOKH was Bishop of Photice in Epirus. Victor, Bishop of Utica, writing in the preface to his *History of the Barbarity of the Vandals* about the year 490, calls himself the pupil of Diadokh, and speaks in high praise of his spiritual writings. Diadokh, therefore, flourished in the second half of the fifth century. His signature appears among those attached to the letter from the Epirote bishops to the Emperor Leo. But nothing more is known of him.

CALLISTUS THE PATRIARCH, a disciple of Gregory the Sinaïte in the *skeet* of Magoola on Mount Athos, led the ascetic life for twenty-eight years in company with one Mark, and especially with Ignatius, with whom he had so great a friendship that "it appeared as though but one spirit was in the two of them." Later, after he had been made Patriarch, he was passing by Mount Athos on his way to Serbia, and during his stay in the Holy Mountain one Maxium foretold his early death. "This *starets* will not see his flock again, for behind him can be heard the funeral hymn, 'Blessed are they that are undefiled in the way.' " On his arrival in Serbia Callistus did, in fact, die. Gregory Palamas, in his treatise on the Jesus Prayer, speaks very highly of the writings of Callistus and Ignatius on the same subject. They lived in the middle of the 14th century.

CHRYSOSTOM. The most famous of the Greek Fathers. He was born about A.D. 345 at Antioch in Syria, and was trained as a lawyer. At the age of thirty-five, however, he was baptized and later ordained. He became Archbishop of Constantinople, in which office he led a life of ascetic simplicity, and was celebrated for his writings and sermons. (The name means "golden-mouthed.") He died in 407.

EPHRAEM THE SYRIAN. The great Syriac writer, poet, and commentator, of the 4th century. He was ordained deacon but in humility refused any higher order. The bulk of his vast output of literary work was written in verse and upon many varieties of theological subjects. He was a notable champion of orthodoxy especially against Marcion and in defence of the creed of Nicaea. He died at Edessa about A.D. 373.

GREGORY PALAMAS. A 14th-century monk of Athos and the outstanding defender on dogmatic grounds of Hesychasm (see SIMEON THE NEW THEOLOGIAN), to which the Council of St. Sophia gave the official approval of the Orthodox Church in 1351. Palamas died as Archbishop of Thessalonika in 1359.

GREGORY THE SINAITE took the habit in the monastery on Mount Sinai about the year 1330. Later he went to Mount Athos, where he stimulated the contemplative life. He also founded three great Lavras in Macedonia, and taught the practice of unceasing prayer. Callistus, the Patriarch of Constantinople, a former pupil of his, wrote his *Life*.

INNOCENT was one of the great Russian missionaries of the 18th century. By the appointment of Peter the Great he was consecrated to be the first Bishop of Pekin, but the Chinese refused to allow the establishment of the bishopric in that city, and Innocent became Bishop of Irkutsk. He laboured as a missionary bishop for some ten years and died at Irkutsk in 1731.

ISIKHI was a native of Jerusalem and in his early years a pupil of Gregory the Theologian. He retired to one of the hermitages in Palestine for some years, but became a priest in the year 412 and established a great reputation as a teacher and interpreter of Holy Scripture. The date of his death is given as 432–433.

JOHN OF DAMASCUS. The famous theologian and hymn-writer who lived in Palestine in the 8th century and honoured in East and West alike. His great work, *The Fountain of Knowledge,* is concerned with religious philosophy and dogmatic theology. A man of immense learning in many fields, he is well known for his three treatises in defence of the "Images" (Icons). One or two of St. John Damascene's very large output of "hymns" are to be found in English Lymn-books, *e.g.,* "Come ye faithful, raise the strain," "The Day of Resurrection," "What sweet of life endureth."

JOHN KARPATHISKY. Nothing certain seems to be known about this writer. But Photius speaks of reading a book which contained, beside writings of Diadokh and Nil, a section by John Karpathisky entitled, "A consoling word to the monks who have turned to Him for consolation from India." This has been taken to imply that he was a contemporary of Diadokh and Nil, and belongs to the fifth century. Karpathos is an island between Rhodes and Crete, and he was presumably either a native of the island or lived there for some time.

KASSIAN THE ROMAN was born between 350 and 360, probably in the neighbourhood of Marseilles. His parents were well-known people and wealthy, and he received a good education. He went to the East and became a monk at Bethlehem. About two years later, hearing of the ascetic achievements of the Egyptian Fathers, he went with a friend, German, to visit them. This was about the year 390. Except for a short visit to their own monastery in 397, the friends stayed among the Egyptian hermits until the year 400. In that year they went to Constantinople, where they were received by St. John Chrysostom, who ordained Kassian deacon and German priest. The two friends were among those who were sent in 405 to Rome by the friends of Chrysostom to seek help for him when he was imprisoned. Kassian did not return to the East, but spent the rest of his life in his native land, still practising the severe asceticism he had learned in Egypt. He left some twelve volumes on the constitution and ordering of the monastic life, written, it is said, at the request of many in whom the monasteries he founded inspired great admiration. He died in 435 and is commemorated by the Orthodox on February 29.

MACARIUS THE GREAT (of Egypt) was the son of a peasant and himself a shepherd. Feeling a strong attraction to the hermit life, he retired to a cell near his own village and later withdrew with some other monks into the desert on the borders of Libya and Egypt. He was ordained priest and became the head of the brotherhood. He suffered at the hands of the Arians for his rigid orthodoxy, and died in the year 390 in the desert at the age of ninety, having spent sixty years in solitude. Miraculous power and the gift of prophecy were attributed to him. He left numerous writings on the spiritual life. His relics are venerated at Amalfi.

MARK THE PODVIZHNIK was one of the most notable of the Egyptian Fathers, but little is known of his life. He is said to have been mild and gentle, to have had such love of the study of Holy Scriptures that he knew both the Old and New Testaments by heart. He is supposed to have lived beyond the age of a hundred years, and to have died at the beginning of the fifth century. He left behind him the memory of his deep spirituality and of his devotion to Holy Communion; but few of the numerous writings ascribed to him have survived.

NICEPHORUS THE RECLUSE was a great ascetic of Mount Athos, who died shortly before 1340. He was the director of Gregory of Salonika (Palamas).

NICETAS STETHATUS was a presbyter of the Studium in the eleventh century, and pupil of St. Simeon the New Theologian, whose virtues and wisdom he absorbed to such an extent that he was said to shine as the twin sun of his teacher.

PHILOTHEUS was *igumen* (abbot) of the Slav monastic community on Mount Sinai, but at what date is not known.

SIMEON THE NEW THEOLOGIAN died in the first half of the eleventh century. He was a monk of the Studium in Constantinople, and a great visionary and mystic. His visions began when he was a boy of fourteen. *The Method* (*i.e.*, the *Hesychast* method of prayer, the way of using the Jesus Prayer) has been attributed to him, but Hausherr gives reasons for concluding that he was not the author, though his influence contributed to the spread of the method. Various explanations of his name have been given, and it has sometimes been translated as "Simeon the Young, the theologian"; but according to Nicetas Stethatus, who wrote his life, the name recalls St. John the Divine, and so would mean "the new St. John." An examination of the whole subject of the *Hesychast* method and its connection with Simeon is to be found in *Orientalia Christiana*, vol. ix, No. 36, June–July, 1927.

ST. JOHN OF THE LADDER, or KLIMAX, lived for forty years in a cave at the foot of Mount Sinai. Then he became Abbot of the Monastery on the Mountain. He died about 600. He wrote a book called *The Ladder to Paradise*, and from this he derives his name. *The Ladder* has been translated into English.

THEOLEPT. A monk of Mount Athos, and later Metropolitan of Philadelphia. Among his pupils at Athos was Gregory Palamas.